CW00434573

Greece & Rome

NEW SURVEYS IN THE CLASSICS No. 30

ROMAN RELIGION

BY

J. A. NORTH

Published for the Classical Association

OXFORD UNIVERSITY PRESS

2000

OXFORD
UNIVERSITY PRESS

Great Clarendon Street, Oxford OX2 6DP

Oxford University Press is a department of the University of Oxford
and furthers the University's aim of excellence in research, scholarship,
and education by publishing worldwide in

Oxford New York

Athens Auckland Bangkok Bogotá Bombay Buenos Aires Calcutta
Cape Town Chennai Dar es Salaam Delhi Florence Hong Kong Istanbul
Karachi Kuala Lumpur Madrid Melbourne Mexico City Mumbai
Nairobi Paris São Paulo Singapore Taipei Tokyo Toronto Warsaw
with associated companies in Berlin Ibadan

Oxford is a registered trade mark of Oxford University Press
in the UK and in cetain other countries

ISSN 0017–3835
ISBN 019–922433–1

Typeset by Joshua Associates Ltd., Oxford
Printed in Great Britain
on acid-free paper by
by Bell and Bain Ltd., Glasgow

CONTENTS

INTRODUCTION

The value of studying ancient religions is not so often challenged today as it used to be: it has become a familiar idea that trying to understand religions requires a comparative approach, that we cannot understand, e.g., Christianity unless we compare it with other religious systems, at least with the other world religions, but also with situations that are quite different – in which religion is not a separate institution on its own, with its own personnel, its own control systems, buildings, ideas and membership, but simply part of the way the society in question works. The religion of the Greeks and Romans in the period before and after the invention of Christianity provides a special kind of foil to our understanding of modern world religions: first, it provides the religious background against which Judaism, Christianity, and eventually Islam first arose, and it deeply influenced their development; secondly, in the period before these religions developed, it provides us with a model of a sophisticated society that had no such autonomous religions at work in it at all. As we shall see the Romans had religious institutions, priesthoods, buildings, sanctuaries; but 'pagan-ism' as a religion in the modern sense simply did not exist until the emergence of Christianity and Judaism forced it to define itself by way of competition; even then the '-ism' suits it very badly, since the pagans never achieved or even tried to achieve the degree of unity or the coherence of doctrine that we today associate with the idea of a religion.

For those who study Roman antiquity for itself, of course, there are other just as compelling reasons for needing to place religion in the life of ancient men and women. Again, there has at times been a comforting assumption that this was not a very necessary part of understanding ancient life. All too often books have been constructed on the assumption that religion was a marginal part of life, interesting perhaps in an antiquarian way, but scarcely needing to be placed at the centre of our understanding. But the fact is that religious activity formed part of every other activity in the ancient world; and so far from placing it in the margin of our accounts, it needs to be assessed at every point, in every transaction. This is more easily said than done: we are accustomed to certain kinds of relationships between religion and other areas of life, including private life; we have certain ideas about the boundaries between what concerns religious life and what is the concern of secular life; and we have ideas about the extent to which politics should intrude or not into religious matters. None of this can be transferred to the ancient world before the establishment of Christianity. The place of religion in Roman society has to be discovered in its own terms.

The survey that follows is concerned to offer a picture of Roman religion and of some of the current debates about its character and development. That picture has changed significantly in the latter decades of the twentieth century, but the problems of interpreting a religion so different from those we today are used to are and will remain an area of profound controversy. The focus of this survey is the religious experience of the Roman people from about the third century BC to the second century AD, which is already sufficently ambitious. It does not attempt to discuss the establishment of Christianity as the main religion of the Empire in the fourth century; nor to do more than survey older theories about the earliest period of Rome as a city. There is one other limitation on its scope: those who follow up the footnotes to this book will very soon find that the evidence behind it consists in part of texts, epigraphic or literary, but also of archaeological evidence in the broadest sense – coins, painting, relief sculpture, the remains of buildings, the topography of the city and many other kinds of physical remains. There is no scope or opportunity to do justice to this material without extensive use of illustrations, charts, and plans and I have not attempted to do that here. A selection will be found in the 'Sources' volume (Vol. II) of Beard, North, and Price, *Religions of Rome* (1998), which also contain many of the texts discussed in this survey. I have referred to them by the system used there, by chapter and item number, in **bold** type (e.g. **1.4a**). There is also now an excellent guide (Claridge (1998)) to the remains of Ancient Rome and a useful dictionary of sites in English (Richardson (1987)) as well as a far more ambitious one in various languages and in progress (Steinby (1993–)).

The bibliography consists for the most part of work in English cited in the footnotes and chosen as the first step towards exploring the subject further. Essential work, particularly recent work, in French and German has been included, and the bibliography also contains some items not cited in footnotes to make it more generally useful in itself. The great handbooks of the subject (in German) are still essential reference works (Wissowa (1912); Latte (1960)). There is now (in French) a very useful brief introduction to the working of the religion and cult by John Scheid (1998b). To check the details of festivals, Scullard (1981) is still useful, though his theories are often out-of-date. Hopkins (1999) is a very recent and entertaining, if idiosyncratic, introduction to pagan, Jewish, and Christian religion under the Empire, with much emphasis on the different varieties of early Christianity.

I am very grateful to Ian McAuslan, the editor of the Survey for *Greece & Rome*, for much advice and assistance from the first conception to the final delivery of this work, also for his endless tolerance, courtesy, and flexibility in dealing with the delays of production. The photograph of a coin is reproduced by courtesy of the Trustees of the British Museum. It will be obvious to readers how much the line of thought in this survey owes to *Religions of Rome* and I happily acknowledge my indebtedness to that seamless collaboration with Mary Beard and Simon Price.

I. THE STORIES OF EARLY ROME

In many ways Roman religion emerges from the standard modern accounts of it as a dry and highly ritualized religion with few if any concessions either to religious self-expression or imagination about the role of gods in the life of men.[1] Historians have tended to associate this character with the success of the Romans in practical aspects of life – warfare, engineering, town-planning – and to suggest that they organized their religious lives with the same kind of brutal efficiency, striking crude bargains with the narrow-minded gods and goddesses that they had themselves created. It will be clear later on that there are some reasons for taking this view, but there are also reasons to think it only a part of the truth, and profoundly misleading if it is mistaken for the whole truth.

One reason for mistrusting the image of the practical Roman is the existence of Roman myths and legends, attributed to the early history of Rome, in which we find traces of some forms of religious behaviour that the Romans later seem to have denied themselves; these also carry with them morals about proper religious behaviour that do not emerge from the type of evidence we have for the later Republican period, or even contradict the evidence about this period. It has sometimes been said that the Romans simply had no mythology of their own and that it was for that reason that they later borrowed the mythology of the Greeks.[2] This is quite true in the sense that they do indeed have no great body of stories on the Greek model about the adventures of their gods and goddesses. In so far as they tell such stories they always seem to reflect Greek myths in Roman guise. If the word myth were restricted to that sense, then we would have to admit that there can have been little trace of an independent creative tradition in early Rome. All the same there are characteristically Roman stories, though mostly disguised as history and placed in historic time.[3]

One clear example of such a story is that of Attus Navius, an early augur who is recorded as having resisted the will of King Tarquinius Priscus (traditional dates: 616–579 BC) when he wanted to carry out a

---

[1] See for instance Warde Fowler (1911).
[2] Latte (1960); Dumézil (1970), 32–59.
[3] For Roman myths in general, Dumézil (1941–5); (1970), 1–78; Grant (1973); Bremmer and Horsfall (1987); Wiseman (1995).

reform in the organization of the cavalry units.[4] Tarquin tested the augur's skills by asking him to say whether he could perform the act of which he (Tarquin) was thinking. Navius said he could perform it and Tarquin announced that he had been thinking of Navius' cutting a whetstone in two with a razor; Navius duly performed the miracle that Tarquin said he was thinking of and the severed whetstone was kept on the site to prove it.. Such miracles were remembered, but no longer really happened in the late Republic. The story must, however, reflect an awareness that such potential actions were part of a priest's role, even if not that of a Roman priest in their own day.

Various of the early kings also have miraculous elements in the stories told about them. Miraculous births and babyhoods are reported in the tradition: Romulus and Remus, most famously, were exposed as babies, but protected and rescued from death by the she-wolf who suckled them.[5] In another version of Romulus' birth,[6] and also in one version of that of Servius Tullius,[7] the sixth king of Rome, a virgin became pregnant miraculously when either a spark or a miraculous phallus penetrated her while she was tending the hearth. Once again this is a miraculous event of a kind, to say the least, outside later Roman parameters. But this particular story seems to have a much closer relationship than the others to the actual practice of religious ritual, because the Vestal Virgins seem in their ritual duties to echo this myth. They had of course to guard their virginity on pain of death; their main responsibility was to look after the hearth and to maintain the sacred fire that symbolized the continuity of Rome; in the secret centre of their cult-place they kept a phallus away from the sight of men. It sounds as though there must have been a close connection between the myth of the king's origins and the symbolic rituals of the Vestals, and that the safety and continuity of the Roman community depended on the ritual maintenance of this founding act of fertilization.[8]

In the case of the deaths of kings there is far less ritual connection in Republican times, though there does seem to have been an early characteristic Latin tradition. The founder kings of Rome (Romulus, the real founder; his ancestor the Trojan hero, Aeneas, whose son Ascanius founded the neighbouring city of Alba Longa; and the King

---

[4] Livy 1.36.2–6 = *RoR* ii.**7.1a**. See Beard (1989).
[5] For the story and its sources, Wiseman (1995), ch. 1.
[6] Plutarch, *Life of Romulus* 2.3–5.
[7] Dionysius of Halicarnassus, *Roman Antiquities* 4.2; Pliny, *Nat. Hist.* 26.204.
[8] See *RoR* i.53–4. For the Vestals, below pp. 19, 24, and Table 1

of the Latins, Latinus), all seem to share a common characteristic. They disappear from the earth in mysterious circumstances and are recognized as gods with a new name. They are not heroes or minor divinities, but high gods of the Romans or the Latins. This is especially clear of Latinus, who becomes Jupiter, under the name Latiaris, and who was the recipient of the special games annually celebrated by the Latin peoples.[9] Romulus becomes Quirinus, one of the three major gods who have their own priests (his was called the *flamen Quirinalis*, similarly to those of Jupiter and Mars, the *Dialis* and the *Martialis*).[10] Aeneas becomes Pater Indiges and although this is for us an obscure figure, there is reason to see him too as a major Roman god, perhaps the sun-god.[11]

The figure in early Rome, however, who most obviously defies the normal principles of Roman behaviour is King Numa, who seems to play the role of the religious founder, and about whom there is a cluster of stories of a miraculous nature. It is as though he was designed to parade all that a model of Roman religious behaviour should *not* be. Yet Numa was the legislator who set up the rules by which the cults of Rome were established; he wrote the books on which all rituals were supposedly based and handed them over to the first ever *pontifex*; he also told the *pontifices* that it was their special job to advise the individual Romans about their religious obligations.[12] In his own life, however, as told by our sources, he was inspired by a nymph, Egeria, with whom he slept and by whom he was given religious advice. On her advice he found a way of luring Jupiter down to the earth from heaven and first enquiring about a ritual procedure and then actually tricking Jupiter into changing the ritual into the form Numa wanted it to take.[13] When Numa's successor King Tullus attempted to repeat this divine experiment, he went wrong and was struck down by Jupiter's own lightning-bolt.[14]

In the Rome we know rather better, the Rome of the late Republican period, such stories as these express religious attitudes that seem never to be found in practice. The life of Cicero is not marked by the sudden irruption of divine forces. Men do not yet become gods – though they

---

[9] Liou-Gille (1980), 176–7.

[10] For the *flamines*, see *RoR* i.28–9; ii.1.3.

[11] Pater Indiges: Liou-Gille (1980), 85–134.

[12] Livy 1.20.5–7 = *RoR* ii.2.

[13] For the story: Ovid, *Fasti* 285–392; Arnobius, *Against the Gentiles* 5.1 (taking the story from a first-century BC historian).

[14] Livy 1.31.5–8; Pliny, *Nat.Hist.* 2.140; 28.14. On the significance of the lightning: Capdeville (1995), 84–95.

are beginning to make extraordinary claims to power and honour. Miracles are not reported. Nobody is said to be struck down by the gods for misbehaviour. Nor are the gods said to have intervened directly in the birth processes even of the most distinguished human beings. Yet we can be reasonably certain that the Romans were aware of stories from early Rome that advertised the possibility of all these things happening. And some of them at least do start to happen in Rome once again in the course of the following century.[15]

There are many different ways of looking at the contrast between the mythical possibilities we have been finding and the living practice of the centuries that followed. One explanation would be to say that the Romans saw the remote past as controlled by different rules from their own time, so that there were possibilities once that no longer existed at later dates. Cicero in the *Republic* hints at a different and more rationalizing view, when he implies that the deification of Romulus was characteristic of an ignorant period.

> His achievements were so great that when he failed to reappear after an eclipse of the sun, he was believed to have been admitted to the number of the gods; a belief that no man has ever been able to attain without an outstanding reputation for virtue. The case of Romulus is the more astounding because other men who were said to have become gods lived in periods of inferior education, when minds were more prone to make inventions and simple folk easily induced to believe in them, whereas Romulus lived less than six hundred years ago . . .   (Cicero, *de rep.* 2.17)

He goes on to describe the culture of Greece in Romulus' time, all on the assumption that deification of men becomes an outdated belief once education has reached a certain point. Today, many find this a sympathetic attitude on the part of Cicero, but we have to recognize that he was not speaking for all his contemporaries. The deification of kings and leaders had become established in the Greek world from the time of Alexander's successors onwards and was on the point of reaching Rome soon after Cicero wrote these words – all too soon, as he would certainly have felt.

There could, however, also be other ways of seeing this relationship between reality and the mythical past. It is easy enough to say that these provide religious elements absent from contemporary life, but do we know that it is true? After all, we do not have to believe and perhaps we should not believe that the sources of information we possess give us a fair or balanced picture of Roman religion even in Cicero's own time, let

---

[15] See below pp. 59–62.

alone for the centuries of Republican history between 500 and 100 BC. Our main sources of information about the earlier centuries are historians such as Livy[16] and Dionysius of Halicarnassus[17] who lived in the age of Augustus (in power from 31 BC–AD 14) and so had no personal knowledge even of the late Republic, let alone of the early years. Their reconstruction of the earlier centuries depended heavily on earlier historians, now lost, who themselves wrote in the second century BC or later still.[18] These are the main sources that provide the outlines of our picture; many others contribute, sometimes crucially – coins that carry religious imagery, the archaeological and topographical record of Rome and its vicinity, inscriptions and especially the Augustan copies of the Roman Calendar. However, it remains true that the overwhelming weight of what texts survive come to us from priestly records or from official sources of one kind or another. The extant evidence generally reflects not the experience of the mass of individual Romans, but the religious activity that affects the state and its activities, above all the doings of magistrates and priests.

The Roman religion we know is based on this limited body of material. It shows a lack of direct divine intervention; a lack of the miraculous; a lack of myths of divine activity; even a lack of individual prophets.[19] Not that we do not have a great deal of divinatory material of one kind or another; but this does not take the form of individuals inspired to tell the truth or predict the future. What we find instead are groups of priests – either *haruspices* (diviners supposedly imported from Etruria) or the priests who guarded the Sibylline Books (called successively the two, the ten, or the fifteen men for sacrifices) – who delivered oracles from their respective knowledge or archives to guide the ritual life of Rome.[20] They essentially reported which of the gods and goddesses needed to receive sacrifices or other forms of ritual appeasement. The *haruspices* brought wisdom from abroad, from Etruria; the *quindecimviri* were the guardians of Greek oracles derived from an ancient prophetess.

There are different ways of understanding this position too. One of these is to accept the sources' picture as a more or less true reflection of

---

[16] On whom see: Miles (1995).
[17] On whom see: Gabba (1991).
[18] Rawson (1976).
[19] North (1990).
[20] On the *haruspices*: MacBain (1982); *RoR* i.19–20; 101–2; ii.7.4; on the Sibylline Books: Parke (1988); *RoR* i.27; 62–3; ii.7.5.

Roman life, to accept that their religion operated with a limited vocabulary of religious elements. Another is to argue that we are being given by our sources a very carefully edited picture of what their religious life was really like, largely chosen to reflect a careful, scrupulous piety. It was a strong element in the Romans' perception of themselves that they were the most religious of all men; this contrasts strangely with many modern perceptions of them as the least religious of all men. But a writer like Livy, who looks back at the Republican period from the period of Augustus, would hardly have been able to detach himself from the assumption that the triumphant success of the Republican Romans in conquering most of the rest of the world that they knew went together with a scrupulous care about the proper worship of the gods. He has been thought by some commentators to be himself a sceptic, though the evidence for this is in fact quite flimsy.[21] But there is no room for doubt that, even if he did have private doubts, his basic narrative carries the message of religious success. On this view it is possible that the religion we find does not reflect reality at all; that Roman religious reality was dense with activities now lost to us.

There are in fact some moments, when we might detect the elements normally excluded from the historians' accounts. Occasionally the state adopts prophetic texts from outside the official collection.[22] Once there was a deliberate policy of confiscating unofficial prophecies.[23] We hear from Cato in his book on agriculture, written in the middle of the second century BC, that a master had to take care to protect his bailiff from putting too much faith in the unofficial astrologers.[24] Magic, again, as in most contexts, is an interesting and challenging case: it is arguable that magical practices and especially charges of magic began to appear in our records only during the early Empire; it is also in that period that we find for the first time a definition and discussion of the origins of magic.[25] Yet it is evident from many incidental references that Italy of the Republican period contained a good deal of activity that we would classify as magical in its character: the enchanting of crops is mentioned in the ancient Roman law-code; human sacrifice, which must be connected with magical practices, was specifically banned in 97 BC by the senate of Rome; and we hear of practitioners of local Italian traditions such as the

---

[21] See below, p. 78.
[22] e.g. during the Hannibalic War, see: *RoR* ii.7.5c.
[23] in 213 BC, *MRR* i.263.
[24] Cato, *On Agriculture* 5.4.
[25] The discussion in Pliny, *Nat. Hist.* 30.1–18.

Marsic snake-charmers.[26] By the late Republic, as we can tell from
Cicero's attacks on some of his contemporaries and from the Roman
poets of the Augustan age, who are fully aware of various, as they see it,
horrific magical practices, the idea has been established that all these
disreputable uses of ritual should be seen as part of a single system, that
is eventually seen as a foreign import. But this whole evolution would
have been impossible, unless there had been diviners and magical
operators, however they were called, who were active in the Republican
period when we hear so little about them.[27]

In the other chapters of this survey, the main preoccupation will be
with areas of religious life about which we have substantial quantities of
information of one kind or another: rituals, religious personnel, festivals,
religious activity in political life, religious buildings and sanctuaries. The
source material for these is quite various – literary, artistic, and
epigraphic sources, as well as coins and the remains of buildings. In
bulk, however, they tell us predominantly about the activities of the
social élites of the Roman world, not about the poorer and less prominent sections of Roman society; they tell us about public activity, more
than private or individual activity; in short, they tell us what the
authorities of Rome would have wanted us to know about, but are far
weaker when it comes to the religion of other groups.

This sets up a fundamental problem about which there has not yet
been as much discussion as there needs to be. How complete is the
picture we get from these materials? One view is that the missing sectors
are not too distorting for us: the emphasis lies on the public sector of
activity because that was the area that mattered to the whole community.
On this view there was no important arena of private religious expression, separate from the public arena, because unlike in a modern
situation the individual citizen did not perceive himself as an isolated
being who needed to consult his or her own conscience, to make his or
her own peace with the gods, or to make life-determining decisions
about his or her religious beliefs and identity. This all represents a
backward projection into the ancient world of a modern consciousness;
so that we would be inventing for the Romans a wholly anachronistic
religious life, which they would not themselves have recognized at all.
The alternative view is that all societies must have certain kinds of
common religious elements, and that one of these must be the personal,

---

[26] For the early code, Crawford (1996), ii.682–4; the ban on human sacrifice is mentioned by
Pliny, *Nat. Hist.* 20.12; for Marsic magicians: Cicero, *On Divination* 1.132.
[27] For discussion, Graf (1997).

emotional experience of anxiety about the supernatural powers that control the working of the universe and desire to influence them. On this view, if we do not hear of this individual experience that can only imply that the evidence is incomplete.

These problems will arise from time to time in what follows and a partial answer to the question will emerge, though there is far from being any certainty. There are certain questions that will need to be borne in mind throughout and it is worth summarizing them here: first, does the evidence that survives give us a fair picture of private as well as public religion? Secondly, does it allow us to see the religious life of the community as a whole, or only that of the dominant class? Thirdly, is it likely that religious activity outside the frame of our sources was so important that our ignorance of it vitiates our whole understanding, or is it likely to be marginal in its effect on the whole?

The myths of early Rome provide only one of a number of clues that the religion of the Romans was less abnormal than it was once thought to have been. But it remains true that, however we may re-interpret and nuance the evidence we have, the public realm of activity seems far more important and far more developed than the religious lives of the individual citizens, men and women, and relatively far more important than in other societies, particularly modern societies. More importantly still, it is hard to resist the idea that private religious experience becomes more important in the course of this period, both inside and outside the experience of Roman pagans. It may be very crude to say that the Roman world became 'more religious' between the Rome that Cicero knew and the Rome Augustine knew, but it certainly is true to say that religious language and reference had penetrated by Augustine's time into areas of life that had once seemed separate from religion and its practice. We shall see in later chapters of this survey that some parts of the development can be reconstructed, but there are many basic issues that still escape analysis, because the materials for discussion hardly exist.

Those later developments leave us with a problem of understanding what had gone before; if it is accepted that the rise of rival religions under the Roman Empire led to a steep rise in the phenomenon of individual religious responsibility at that time, how should we consider the religious attitudes of earlier generations? There are at least two distinct possibilities: first, that pagans were in general indifferent about their religious activities; secondly, that pagans had far less sense of an individual relationship to the gods and conceived themselves far more as part of a community and hence as automatically part of its religious activities. If you grow up assuming that religious needs are not an individual matter at all, but an expression of the state of the whole city of which you are part, to be met by city action taken on the citizens' behalf by their leaders, then you will not feel the religious inadequacies that modern commentators, thinking from an implicit Christian stand-point, have so often assumed that a Roman must have felt. We shall consider later on the circumstances that may have brought about this change of self-perception.[28]

[28] See below, ch. VII.

II. THE EARLY CHARACTER OF ROMAN RELIGION

The fundamental principle on which the religion of the Romans used to be interpreted was the idea that the Romans were an unusually conservative society. In some respects, this is perfectly true: we can for instance show that some of the rituals that were still being practised regularly in the first century BC, and even later than that, were already in place in the sixth century BC;[1] again we know from later Roman orators such as Cicero that they placed a great emphasis on the ancestral customs and ways of the Roman people (the *mos maiorum*) and it is a reasonable guess that this was not a new idea in Cicero's day but a long-cherished attitude;[2] again, it is quite clear that the Romans placed a great deal of emphasis on getting their rituals precisely right in every detail, so that the slightest error invalidated the whole ceremony of which it formed part.[3] If so, and if they did this year after year, there should have been no change at all. How could conservatism be taken further?

Working from this supposed conservatism, scholars in the nineteenth and early twentieth centuries developed theories that explained the particular characteristics of the whole religious system on the basis that it long retained a special 'Roman-ness' that could be traced back to remote periods even perhaps before the city itself was founded in the eighth century BC. This idea was combined with a more generally accepted theory derived particularly from the anthropology of the late nineteenth and very early twentieth century, which traced all human religions back to a common stage called 'animism', in which worship was devoted not to gods or goddesses as known to later periods but to powers residing in nature or in the activities of nature – in streams, woods, the growing crops, anywhere that natural activity was to be seen.[4] Later on, following the theory, these abstract powers came to be seen more and more as having the form and even behaviour of humans

---

[1] See, for example, Dumézil (1970), 83–8.
[2] See, for example, the opening of Cicero's speech, *On his House*: to say that an institution was ancestral was automatically to praise it.
[3] North (1976).
[4] Warde Fowler (1911), 114–168; Rose (1948); Latte (1960), 36–63; for discussion, *RoR* i.10–18; ii.2–4; North (1997).

or even animals, so that they took on human or animal appearance, could be represented in statues or other artistic forms, and became the subjects of stories and adventure. In other words, they become progressively more like the gods and goddesses we associate with Greeks, Romans and many other peoples of the ancient – and modern – world.[5]

This theory seemed at the time to be very illuminating about the experience of the early Romans in particular, and so the idea of a 'pre-deistic phase' became a normal part of the vocabulary of debate on the subject.[6] As a matter of fact, the Romans do seem to have had a long period during which they made no representations of their gods and goddesses, or at least that is what they themselves thought.[7] Some of the gods and goddesses seem never to have appeared in human guise. Even when they did so, there seem to have been no specifically Roman stories about Jupiter, Juno, Minerva and the rest; when the Roman poets and dramatists tell such stories, they seem in general to be Greek stories borrowed rather than native ones of their own. The fact that Roman gods and goddesses are often closely identified with Greek ones (Jupiter with Zeus; Juno with Hera; Minerva with Athena and so on) encourages the idea that the Greek ones came first and that the Roman ones were just later imitations.[8]

As a result of all this, the theory became very well established that Roman conservatism had caused a very characteristic religious history for the Romans of the early period. They had long retained the animistic character of primitive religion and had only come belatedly and under the influence of their Etruscan neighbours to move on to the next stage of 'anthropomorphism', that is of perceiving the gods in human form. It was thought that Rome provided an interesting example of a stunted development along the lines of other ancient peoples, but failing to reach the level of the Greeks from whom they therefore needed to borrow in the effort to catch up with the norm.[9]

The theory then develops yet another layer. One consequence of the

---

[5] The development of the gods: Warde Fowler (1911), 145–64.

[6] Still influential, for instance, in Scullard (1981).

[7] According to Varro (fr. 13 and 18 (Cardauns), from Augustine, *Civitas Dei* 4.31), the period lasted down to c.575 BC, which is in fact approximately the date at which Etruscan influence is being felt in Rome. See *RoR* ii.1.1a; but it is not clear how this information could have come down to Varro's time.

[8] For the gods and their Greek equivalents, see below, Table 3. For an apparent early identification of a Roman deity (Vulcan) with a Greek one (Hephaestus), see Coarelli (1983–5), i.161–78; *RoR* ii.1.7c(ii).

[9] e.g. Warde Fowler (1911), 1–23.

strange development of Roman religion is that it placed all its emphasis not on the gods or myths, still less on the meaning of religious actions, but purely on rituals and their accurate repetition. A combination of this excessive ritualism and the domination of the system by priests, whose main purpose and main expertise lay exactly in the area of recording and repeating ritual actions, led to the erosion of significance in the whole activity. The people lost any belief in the deities and simply accepted that the actions of priests, which they did not understand and did not need to understand, conducted all the negotiations with the divine inhabitants whose favour would insure Roman success in war and in peace.[10] So this whole complex of theories gave an overall picture of an almost wholly negative and depressing type. The religion had once had its validity in the very early days of Roman experience, before or just after the foundation of the actual city. But it had always been backward and primitive; it soon lost touch with its agricultural and pastoral roots; it soon enough came to be dominated by priests whose only interest lay in the mindless repetition of formulae, that became more and more meaningless as the context in which they belonged grew remote from the experience of an urban population.

It is always a dangerous situation when a theory becomes so well established that it begins to escape fundamental criticism; the theory described above had a long history, even though many of its details were the objects of sustained criticism and debate.[11] Today, little if any of it could be defended. Partly, this is because the evolutionary scheme of development that underpinned the theories had long since been abandoned by anthropologists; this in fact cut the ground from under the feet of the ancient historians, though it was a long time before they realized what had happened to them. But there were also obvious facts that the theory ignored – for instance, that the names of the Roman gods and even the Latin word for a god (*deus*, *dea*) go back to Indo-European roots and that must imply that the Romans had had gods from the city's very foundation, indeed far earlier than that. So much for an animistic or pre-deistic phase.

At the same time, the archaeology of sixth-century Rome has produced stronger and stronger evidence that Rome at this stage was far from being an isolated community, developing its own traditions. They were in close contact with other peoples who undoubtedly

---

[10] Warde Fowler (1911), 270–91.
[11] See, for example, the work of Koch (1937); (1960); Altheim (1938).

influenced their cultural development – their Etruscan neighbours to the North; the Carthaginians, who were themselves in touch with some of the Etruscan cities; but above all the Greeks, who were supplying artefacts for the Italian markets, but some of whom were also living and working in the vicinity of Rome.[12] It is not necessary to think that Roman culture was ever completely dominated or controlled by Etruscans or by any other of the local ethnic groups; the survival of the Latin language proves the continuing independence of Rome and her Latin neighbours, but they were part of a quite cosmopolitan cultural exchange with other parts of the Mediterranean world.[13] There is now ample evidence to show that the idea of a purely Roman tradition, unaffected by foreign influence and detectable by its character at any date, should be treated as no more than a modern myth.

One of the most effective critics of the theory long before it was generally abandoned was the controversial Indo-Europeanist Georges Dumézil. He studied the mythology and theology of the different peoples and societies where Indo-European languages were spoken from antiquity onwards, in an effort to prove that a common structure underlay all these traditions.[14] He argued that the common structure was derived from the characteristic social structure of the original speakers of the language from which the others are descended. He found in Rome a prime example of the triadic structure of three functions (Rulers; Warriors; Farmers) characteristic, as he thought, of all Indo-European groups. In particular, he argued powerfully that this fundamental conception (which he called the *idéologie* of the Indo-Europeans) can be discovered in the original triad of Roman gods (Jupiter, Mars, and Quirinus) and in the myths of the first four Kings (Romulus and Numa represent two aspects of the first function (authority and law); Tullus the second function (war), and Ancus Marcius the third (production)).[15] This theory is in itself highly debatable, not just in its impact on our understanding of Rome, but also in its wider Indo-European form, not least because our knowledge of Indo-Europeans is derived entirely from the evidence of language, but Dumézil's theories assume that we can attribute other common characteristics to the speakers of

---

[12] Cornell (1995), 198–214; Holloway (1994); *RoR* ii ch. 1.

[13] Cornell (1995), 151–72.

[14] Dumézil (1941–5); (1968–73).

[15] Dumézil (1970), 60–82;

these languages.[16] Much of his work on Roman religion is often regarded as creative and suggestive, but insecure in its theoretical base; however, this does not affect his arguments against the animistic theory, the proposition that the vocabulary of gods and of particular gods was part of Rome's inheritance at the earliest date.

The implications of this shift are radical for the subject, because it removes a key organizing principle of our understanding. The existence of a primitive, characteristically Roman tradition that survived into later times and was eroded gradually by foreign influences in the course of the third and second centuries BC was the foundation on which the whole narrative account of the early religion was built. Its disappearance from the argument leaves us without any secure basis on which to build a new account. One option is to reverse the procedure and start from the end not the beginning, working backwards from what we know relatively well and towards what we know so inadequately.

The approach followed in this survey is therefore to look at the structure of the main institutions as we meet them in the material of the late Republic and the early principate. The most obvious assumption to make might be that this will provide us with an outline that could be assumed safely to fit any period. However, this is not at all the conclusion that seems to emerge from the evidence. Much of what follows suggests, not that there was some timeless character that remained unchanged through the centuries, but rather that religious institutions were very much influenced by change in other areas of society and especially by major changes in the political system. We know of a series of major points of change in Roman life over the course of Regal, Republican and early Imperial history. The most obvious of them are the creation of the Republican system after the expulsion of the last king; the collapse of the Republican system in the years down to 49 BC; and the establishment of the Imperial regime in the age of Augustus down to AD 14. There must also have been other great turning points, less obvious in their impact, at the end of the fourth century BC, when many scholars have argued that the Republican system was radically reformed as Rome's power expanded in Italy;[17] and after the Hannibalic war in the late third century BC as Rome's power expanded into the whole Mediterranean world.

It will become obvious from later chapters that at least one of these

---

[16] Good discussion in Scheid (1983); Momigliano (1984b); Belier (1991).
[17] Cornell (1995), 369–90.

political turning points corresponds very closely to a profound change in religious life as well. In that one case we have enough detailed information to trace and prove the correspondence: as the Republican system weakened in the first century BC, so the religious institutions were transformed into an instrument of the new monarchic order, rather than an expression of republicanism. To prove correspondence is far easier than to establish the direction of causality, but perhaps the question of what caused what is not the most important one to ask. We shall see that by the middle Republican period, the institutions of religion have come to fit the Republican order of the time; that order vanishes in just a few years as Augustus appropriates the key positions and offices for himself and his family.[18]

This pattern of development cannot be any accident and indeed may be seen as part of a wider characteristic of Roman religious life in this period. It is not just political life in which religious structures and the other institutions of society have a close relationship. In a sense, all social formations in Rome have religious aspects to them. So clubs and colleges are dedicated to a particular deity and have priests as well as other leaders (*magistri*);[19] local communities have their own cults and rituals; and families (or at least property-owning families) have their own religious activities, in the charge of the *paterfamilias*, that is the head of the extended Roman family,[20] including all his male descendants of whatever age and also the women, whether his descendants or not, unless they are members of another such extended family; his authority also extended to the members of the *familia* in an even wider sense including the slaves and freedmen of the estate.[21] On his estate, he is responsible for religious rituals as for all other aspects of farm life; in Cato's handbook on farming, his very first duty is:

Whenever the *paterfamilias* visits the farm, after he has first greeted the Lar of the household, he should go round the property, on the same day if possible.

(Cato, *On Agriculture* 2)

But he also controls the religious activity of the farm manager, who must not for instance conduct religious ceremonies or consult soothsayers without the master's authority.[22] As in law, so in religion, it is the master who is the effective actor for the group.

[18] Below, pp. 33–4.
[19] For *collegia*, see *RoR* i.42; 272.
[20] *RoR* i.48–9.
[21] On the Roman notion of *familia*, see Gardner (1998).
[22] Cato, above ch. I, n. 24.

The same pattern can be seen in relation to the activity of women in religious life. They seem to have had no active role in the traditional cultic life of the Romans.[23] They were not eligible to hold any priesthood any more than any magistracy, so that all part in religious authority was closed to them in civic life.[24] In family life, as we have seen,[25] the active role seems to have lain entirely with the *paterfamilias,* on whose death the women of the family could inherit a share of the property, but never the role of *paterfamilias.* As we have already seen in other areas of religious life, this Roman reality seems to be challenged by myths, in which women do play strong roles as religious creators, for instance Egeria, Numa's adviser, or the prophetess who brings the Sibylline Books to Rome; so they are also by the role of the Vestal Virgins, which is paradoxically central to the city's whole religious life.[26]

What appears significant is that in the later Republic there seem to be the first signs of some change in this traditional religious role, just as there is some movement towards a freer role for women in Roman life in general, though no real trace of any role of authority for them. The change, if it is one, happens in the context of an old cult in a new guise, probably under Greek influence. The Romans themselves called it the 'Greek' cult of Ceres and it was dedicated to Ceres and her daughter Proserpina, the Mother and the Maiden.[27] We see this reflected in a Sibylline oracle that gives directions for rituals and processions in which women, groups of older and younger women, take the leading ritual roles.[28] The rituals in question seem to go back to the period between the two great Punic Wars and we know of their practice down to the late Republic. Cicero even makes room for them in his speculative religious code in his *On the Laws,* which shows precious little other sign of religious activity by women.[29]

If the general conclusion of this chapter is correct, then the religion of the Romans at different times reflects quite accurately the political and social conditions of the society and its formations at the relevant times. One of the implications of this is that change may have happened at a far faster rate than is usually allowed for. If so, then it may be unacceptable to argue back from the religion we know reasonably well in the third-first

---

[23] Scheid (1992b).
[24] For their activities, Kraemer (1992), 50–70.
[25] Above, p. 18; see also below, p. 74.
[26] Vestals: Beard (1980); (1995); Staples (1998); *RoR* i.51–4.
[27] Le Bonniec (1958), 379–462.
[28] For the text, *RoR* ii.7.5a.
[29] *On the Laws* 21 cf.37.

centuries BC to any earlier period. The next chapter will look in more detail at the possibilities of tracing a historical development; but in the meantime, scepticism about how good a picture we have of the earlier periods remains very much in point.

III. THE RELIGION OF REPUBLIC AND EMPIRE

The Republic is the name we use to describe the characteristic political system of the Romans from the fall of the monarchy until the establishment of the new, though disguised, monarchy of Augustus and his successors. It is a system that we know quite well from its last century or so, because the writings of Cicero, Caesar, and Sallust as well as those of many others survive from that period. From the earlier years of the Republic we have only the historical tradition preserved by Livy and Dionysius of Halicarnassus, both of whom wrote in the period of Augustus; their tradition is in fact dependent on earlier writers, but even these only take us back to the middle of the second century BC at the earliest.[1] There is therefore a great gap between the creation of the system in the late sixth century BC and the recording of it at least three centuries later. For the most part what follows describes the situation in the second and first centuries; how far the picture can safely be projected backwards into earlier centuries is, as we have seen, very much an open question. Given the Romans' reluctance to make basic changes in their institutions, it would not be surprising if the evolution from the monarchic system of archaic Rome to the developed Republican system we know took some generations to achieve.

The basic principles of the political system are:

1. that final decisions are taken by popular votes in assemblies functioning according to very complicated rules;
2. that no individual has power on his own or for more than a short period, and then only when elected to that power by an assembly;
3. that policy is decided between the elected magistrates and the senate, consisting of ex-magistrates who become life members.

In theory, this system shares the power between elected magistrates, life senators, and popular assemblies and late Republican sources do speak of it as a mixed constitution, a mixture of oligarchic, monarchic, and democratic elements.[2] But in practice much authority and control, and almost all policy initiative, lay with the members of a limited number of wealthy families, who alone were eligible for election and as a result

---

[1] Rawson (1976); Cornell (1995), 1–30; Miles (1995).
[2] So, Polybius, book 6; Cicero, *Republic* 1.

controlled all the initiatives in politics, foreign policy, and war. There is much controversy between historians as to how far these families were the real rulers of Rome, how far they had to take account of lower-class voters, who had great power at least in theory to determine the great issues of any period; and also how large the group of families was that had access to these offices, over long periods of time.[3] Was this group a fixed tiny élite? Or did it change from decade to decade? There are strong arguments for thinking that it did change from generation to generation, but slowly enough for contemporaries to perceive it as almost a fixed order. In the words of the historian Sallust,[4] when commenting on Marius' hesitation before standing for the consulship:

At that time, while citizens of low rank could attain to the other offices, the consulship was passed through the hands of one noble into those of another. There was no new man so famous or so outstanding in his deeds that he would not be thought unworthy of that honour, as if polluted.

What is not in doubt is that these same families, who certainly monopolized political office also monopolized the important priesthoods. The Romans themselves were certainly aware of this and even proud of it.[5]

Among the many institutions, members of the college of *pontifices*, created and established by our forbears under the inspiration of the gods, nothing is more famous than their decision to commit to the same men both the worship of the gods and the care of state interests; the result was that the most illustrious citizens might assure the upholding of religion by the proper administration of the state and the upholding of the state through the careful interpretation of religion.   (Cicero, *de domo* 1)

There is therefore a precise sense in which religion and politics are in the closest association in Republican Rome; but this is also true in a wider sense, as we shall see by examining the priestly colleges in more detail.

The first striking fact to be noticed from Table 1 is the number and complexity of these priesthoods. So far as we can tell they almost all go back to very early times and only one is specifically invented in the Republican period. They all have quite precise duties and we do not ever hear of demarcation disputes between them. Traditionally, they chose their own members, conducted their own rituals, made their own decisions, and kept their own records. As the chart makes clear, they

---

[3] Hopkins and Burton, in Hopkins (1983); Millar (1984).
[4] *Jugurthine War* 63.6–7.
[5] For the facts, Szemler (1972); *RoR* i .99–108.

TABLE 1: *Priests in Rome*

---

1. Four major colleges of priests

Pontifices:

9 members from 300 BC, five plebeian, four patrician; increased to 15 members by Sulla; members co-opted by the College until *lex Domitia* and again from Sulla until 63 BC; at other dates elected by 17/35 tribes on the nomination of existing members of the Colleges.

Head: the *pontifex maximus,* who speaks for the College in the senate, and chooses and disciplines the additional members.

Additional members:
Flamines (3 major ones – *Dialis, Martialis, Quirinalis* – and 12 minor)
Rex sacrorum (1 – successor to the original King (*rex*))
Vestal Virgins (6, serving for thirty years from childhood)

Functions: advisers to the senate about all matters concerned with the *sacra*; advisers to the people on matters of sacred law, including burial law. Supervisors over matters of family law (adoption, inheritance etc.); keepers of records.

Augures:

Numbers etc. as *pontifices,* but no additional members.

Election/co-optation as for *pontifices.*

Functions: supervisors of and advisers about all the rituals and procedures concerned with the auspices.

Duo/decem/quindecimviri sacris faciundis:

Originally 2; 10 from 367 BC; 15 after Sulla.

Election/co-optation as for *pontifices.*

Functions: care of and, though only when asked by the senate, consultation of the Sibylline Books.

Tres/septemviri epulones:

College created as three members in 196 BC; increased to 7 by Sulla.

Election/co-optation as for *pontifices,*

Functions: supervision of the regular Games in Rome.

2. Priestly groups sometimes consulted by the senate

Fetiales:

20.

Functions: deal with matters of relationship with other states – war, peace, treaties etc.

Haruspices:

Later on, list of 60.

Functions: not a Roman college, at least in the Republican period: either specialists in Etruscan lore of prodigies, lightnings, other divination etc.; or lower-class experts on the reading of entrails at sacrifice.

TABLE I (*cont.*):

---

3. Groups never consulted by the senate

Salii:

2 groups of 12 each.

Functions: ritual dancing and chanting through the city at March and October Festivals.

Luperci:

2 groups – numbers not known.

Functions: running through city at Festival of Lupercalia, striking passers-by with thongs of goatskin.

Fratres Arvales:

12.

Functions: maintaining the cult of dea Dia, at a grove outside Rome. Much involved with the cult of the Emperors after the Augustan revival.

---

had a very diverse range of duties, from appearing for a specific festival once a year at one extreme, to being responsible for numbers of public rituals and records at the other. The most complex and in some ways most important was the college of the *pontifices*; the college consisted not only of the *pontifices* proper but the *rex* (sacred king), the *flamines* and the six Vestals. We know that these priests and priestesses attended meetings and dinners, but not what part they played in the decision-making of the college. The *rex* was said to have been the replacement for the real king when the monarchy was abolished in about 509 BC; but the leader of the college in Republican times was the senior *pontifex* (called the *pontifex maximus*), who spoke on the college's behalf and acted for it on ritual occasions. He also had some limited authority over the other members of his college.[6]

Together with the *augures* and the *fetiales*, they served as the expounders of the sacred law on different topics to the senate. So in 191 BC, for example, there was a dispute about the proper way in which the ritual of war declaration should be carried out. The *fetiales* were consulted:

The consul, acting on the decree of the senate, referred to the college of the *fetiales* the issue of whether the war should be declared directly to King Antiochus or whether it would be enough for it to be announced at some frontier post . . .The *fetiales* replied that they had already given a ruling, when consulted about the war aginst King Philip, to the

---

[6] For the *pontifex maximus*: *RoR* i.55–8; 107–8; 186–9.

effect tht it made no difference whether the war was declared to him directly or at a
frontier-post.   (Livy 36.3.7–9)

All the major colleges seem to have been in this way the experts on some
area of sacred law. The *augures* have however by far the most politically
effective powers of this kind. In fact Cicero in the *On the Laws* seems to
give them alarmingly wide powers:

And whatever an augur shall declare to be unjust, unholy, harmful, or ill-omened shall
be null and void. And if anyone fails to obey, it shall be a capital offence.
                                                   (Cicero, *On the Laws* 2.21)

It is important to remember here: first, that Cicero himself held the
augurate and was very proud of it; secondly, that the *On the Laws* was
not describing the real situation at the time, but recommending the best
way of doing things on the basis of Roman practices.[7] Clearly, we should
not rely on Cicero as a guide to the realities on this question. In fact the
augurs could only make recommendations to the senate if asked to; and
only the senate could declare a law null and void, though they did it on
the advice of the augurs. All the same, the powers of the college did
enable them to sit in judgement on laws that the assemblies had passed
and it is fair to see them as a constitutional committee in a key position
when there was controversial legislation under debate.[8] The other
colleges have less dramatic powers, though the *duo/decem/quindecimvir*i
at least control an important political asset in the Sibylline Books, whose
oracles sometimes play their part in a political battle.[9]

Two important points emerge from this survey:

1. Religious authority within the colleges is very widely spread: the
   different colleges have different tasks and do not interfere in one
   another's areas of responsibility; the members share the college's
   responsibilities amongst themselves and the number of members
   increases over time; so, the *pontifex maximus* may have somewhat
   more influence than his colleagues, but he has to consult them and
   consider their views and can even be over-ruled by them. In no sense
   was he, in the Republican period at least, the head of the state
   religion.

2. The different colleges have very different degrees of influence in
   political life: from the *augures* and the *pontifices* who have great

---

[7] *On the Laws* – Rawson (1973b).
[8] Linderski (1986), esp 2180–4.
[9] For example, when in 56 BC an oracle affected who should restore the king of Egypt: Dio
Cassius 29.15.1–16; Cicero, *To his Friends* 1.7.4 = 18.4 (Shackleton Bailey).

influence to the *septemviri* – let alone the minor colleges – is a great step. Yet all the four major colleges recruit their members from very highest level of the ruling élite.

When we consider the rules of the colleges, the careful, conscious avoidance of any concentration of power becomes even clearer. Each college normally contained no more than one member of any family or clan; so, for instance, a father was rarely if ever succeeded by his son in his own lifetime. Secondly, and even more significantly, it was very rare for any individual to hold more than one major priesthood.[10] The result of this was that control over religion was very widely disseminated through the aristocratic families and it was extremely difficult for any individual to exercise control to any significant extent over the making of religious decisions. This tendency is deliberately increased as time goes on, by the gradual increase in the number of priesthoods, which seems to have started at fewer than ten, but finished at over fifty. So more and more élite members shared the privilege or power.[11]

All the same, it becomes very clear in the late Republican period that the membership of the colleges was a matter of very great public interest and concern. It would therefore be quite wrong to conclude that religious influence was so widely distributed that the individual's role became unimportant. There was in fact a sustained argument about the role that the assemblies should or should not play in the selection of priests: first, as early as the third century BC, the *pontifex maximus* came to be elected from amongst the *pontifices* by a section (just less than half) of the whole people of Rome.[12] A series of laws passed or proposed between 145 BC and 63 BC concerned the mode of selection of all priests of the major colleges and the sequence of laws makes it clear that this was a highly controversial matter, hard to settle and repeatedly disputed. The old system was that the colleges co-opted new members to replace dead colleagues at their own discretion and by their own methods. A proposal for change failed in 145 BC,[13] but succeeded in 104 BC through the law of Domitius Ahenobarbus, a tribune in that year.[14] The new system did not allow free elections because the nomination of the candidates was left with the priests of the college,

---

[10] North (1990); *RoR* i.103–4. There is a small number of exceptions, not surprisingly considering that these were conventions not fixed rules, until the legislation of the late Republic.
[11] See above Table 1.
[12] Cicero, *On the Agrarian Law of Rullus* 2.16 and 18.
[13] Cicero, *Laelius* 96; *MRR* i.470.
[14] *MRR* i.559–60; Rawson (1974); North (1990); *RoR* i.135–7.

who were no doubt careful which candidates they allowed on the list: but the tribes had a final say according to the same special procedure as had long existed for the *pontifex maximus*. This new system was abolished in Sulla's legislation, but the number of priests also increased; presumably, the idea was to reduce the level of competition while excluding the popular element.[15] This was again reversed in 63 BC by another tribunician law.[16]

One question raised by this sequence of events is why so much was at stake in the political issue of the membership of the major priestly colleges. They certainly took a part in the decision-making processes of the republican system, though it is not a final and determinative part. Table 2 illustrates the relationship as it emerges from our sources for the third–first centuries BC. Business is initiated in the Senate, either on the basis of reports received, or as a result of the actions of magistrates or occasionally on issues raised by the priests. If the senate judges that there is a point on which they require the priests to make a recommendation, it is they who refer the matter to the priests. They follow traditional rules in doing this: matters of war and peace to the *fetiales* (as we saw above), prodigies to the *haruspices* or to the *decem-/quindecimviri sacris faciundis* and so on.

The colleges reported back to the senate and seem to have had no power to reach an independent decision or act on their own initiative. On the other hand, their judgements about the sacred law or the interpretations they offer were respected by the senate in taking their decisions. But it is clear that if the senate did not refer an issue at all, the matter remained unresolved. These issues become fairly clear in the celebrated case of Cicero's house. We have the speech of Cicero (*de domo*) in which he actually pleads his case in the college of *pontifices*; he claimed that the action of Clodius in consecrating part of his house to the goddess Libertas (Freedom) was not binding because of irregularities in the procedure. When they had heard the pleadings, the college reported to the senate, confirming that there had been such irregularities. On the strength of this advice the senate, not the college, authorized the return of the house to Cicero, though Cicero makes quite clear that in the senate's debate, an important influence was exercised by the members of the college (almost all of them) who were also priests. Each gave his own view.[17]

---

[15] *MRR* ii.75.
[16] Dio Cassius 37.1–2. *MRR* ii.167–8.
[17] Cicero, *Letters to Atticus* 4.2 = 74 (Shackleton Bailey).

TABLE 2: *Religious Action in Rome: The Handling of Prodigies in the Second Century B.C.*

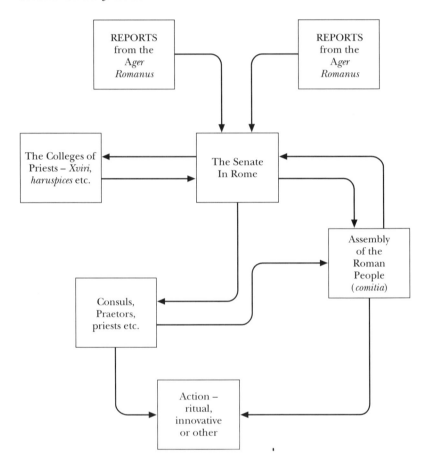

It is perhaps going too far to say that the senate was the main decision-making body in the Roman religious order, but it certainly was playing a central and co-ordinating role.[18] On its instructions, the magistrates or priests or other groups carried out sacrifices or took vows or perform other rituals. The most important conclusion, however, is not that the senate was dominant, but that religious authority was so widely dis-seminated through the governing élite, whether as magistrates, or priests, or senators. Even the popular assemblies played a limited part,

---

[18] For this argument see especially Beard (1990).

before acquiring control of the elections, because certain transactions required the authority of the people and were not valid without it.[19] However this distribution of authority may have felt to the participants at the time, it seems that the theory, whether expressed or not, was thoroughly republican and must have developed over the centuries in parallel with the political system.

This analysis of the role of the colleges has not provided any simple answer to the question why priesthoods were so valuable to Roman politicians: it has often been thought that there is one very obvious answer. One of the most strongly held views about the character of Roman religion, ever since it became an object of specific study at all in the early nineteenth century, is that its period of success was in the most archaic periods and that by the end of the Republican period it had long been in a deep decline, drained of real significance, polluted by foreign invasions of cults and rituals and reduced to a mere set of devices retained for the convenience of political operators of different kinds. So, the view taken of priesthood was that it had become nothing more or less than a political office, whose value lay in its ability to interfere in political conflicts.[20] In part, it is quite clear that this view of Roman religion has always rested on misunderstandings of the nature of their tradition and its practices. There has been too close a modelling of pagan religion on the expectations of modern Christians and consequently a tendency to see any non-Roman influence as a sign of failure or weakness, in the same way as a non-Christian influence (or a non-Protestant influence) would be interpreted as a sign of weakness in a Christian context.[21] The Romans themselves, as we shall see later, were perfectly willing to accept a good deal of change, introduced from abroad, and seem to have perceived such developments as a source of strength not of weakness.

Where foreign influence is concerned, we can be quite confident that past interpretations were misdirected. When it comes, however, to the relations of politics and religion, there are somewhat more delicate problems to be discussed, before we can be sure of the ground. It is beyond doubt that religion was deeply involved in Roman political life at all periods we know about. This was inevitable if only because religious rituals were so closely intertwined with all other activities of war and of peace. So, for instance, the passing of a law or the electing of

---

[19] The decision over Clodius illustrates the point: Clodius' dedication was ruled invalid precisely because he was not specifically authorized by a popular vote. For other examples *RoR* i.105–8.
[20] So, Taylor (1961), 76–97; Szemler (1972).
[21] North (1976).

a magistrate both involved the taking of auspices before the assembly met; the validity of these auspices was a matter that fell within the jurisdiction of the *augures*, who were responsible for the special system of rules that controlled them (the *ius augurale*).[22] As has already been mentioned, this does not imply that they can invalidate laws or elections by their own act; but they can be used like a constitutional committee to offer rulings on difficult points. In fact, in the late Republic such problems do arise more than once. A famous example was the very controversial legislation of the early 50s BC, where the opponents of Caesar and his allies repeatedly tried to establish that the whole programme should be invalidated and cancelled because of a religious objection to its validity.[23]

The issue at stake here is not the existence or interest of these powers, but the way in which they were used. The extreme form of the 'decline' hypothesis would imply that the powers were used purely for the political advantage of the augurs, or of a majority of them, with no regard for the actual state of the augural law. In fact, there are two possible variations of this view: first, that all élite Romans were complete sceptics who were in a conspiracy to deceive other sections of the population; secondly, that the whole population was sceptical and the religious law understood universally to be a meaningless set of rules, maintained only for exploitation in political conflict. The second view is quite impossible, if only because élite members normally speak in public with careful respect about the gods; the first, the conspiracy theory, cannot by its nature be refuted and has at least the support of a famous passage in the Greek historian Polybius speaking of Rome as he knew it in the 140s BC, where he implies that the Romans were superior to the Greeks precisely because their leaders still do what the Greek leaders have forgotten to do, use the masses' superstitions to keep them in subjection; but he immediately goes on to destroy his own view, by asserting that Roman magistrates always kept their oaths.[24] So, even on his view, it is not just the masses but the magistrates who are profoundly respectful towards their religious obligations and in this respect far superior, on his view, to their Greek contemporaries who had forgotten these lessons.

An example will help here. Part of the famous conflict, mentioned above, between Clodius and Cicero in the middle 50s BC, turned on

---

[22] On which see Linderski (1986).
[23] *RoR* i.126–9.
[24] Polybius 6.56.6–14 = *RoR* ii.13.

Clodius' action, while Cicero was in exile, in consecrating part of Cicero's house to the goddess Libertas (Liberty) – both making his house into a sacred building so he could not restore it; and referring, with savage wit, to the fact that Cicero had been exiled for violating the rights and Liberty of a Roman citizen, when he put a number of them to death without a trial at the end of his consulship in 63 BC.[25] Both Cicero's speech on the subject and the references to Clodius' own statements about the issue treat the religious question with great seriousness; but they are also engaged in a major political conflict; it must always be possible that these two particular opponents were totally cynical in their use of religious methods and arguments and interested only in control over the property. However, the very public conflict makes no sense at all unless there was a widespread feeling that it was important that the issue should be properly resolved and dangerous if the consecration were reversed without proper legal rulings taking place. The final decision, as Cicero mentions in a letter to Atticus, had to be made at the very centre of Roman political life – in the senate.[26]

The idea that the whole college of *pontifices* and the whole Roman senate were engaged in a religious charade carried out for the benefit of the superstitious masses seems as unlikely as any hypothesis can be. It also seems to rest on a profound mistake: the underlying idea has to be that, as Roman nobles became more educated and sophisticated, they easily turned away from belief in the gods and towards some form of scientific materialism, believing that the universe could be explained without recourse to the gods. But this assumption is an anachronistic one: easy scientific rationalism may be available in our time but it was not in theirs. There were some philosophical systems that disposed of the gods or marginalized them, and some of the Roman élite certainly understood or followed such systems; but to jump from that to the assumption that the élite were all scientific rationalists exploiting the ignorant masses is quite without any justification.[27]

It is also easy to forget, while concentrating on aspects of religious life in which historians, both ancient and modern, have thought to find evidence of Roman neglectfulness of their traditions, that in many ways late Republican Romans were very careful and concerned about their

---

[25] Cicero, *On his House* and *On the Response of the Haruspices*, provide much discussion of the issues, though entirely from Cicero's point of view. On the cult of Libertas, Weinstock (1971), 133–45.

[26] Above n. 17.

[27] Though Epicurean philosophers did come close to this position; for Epicureanism in Rome, see Sedley (1998).

religious life and convinced that it was a source of great strength to them. It is possible to see this concern in action at several different levels of activity. One is the theological level: this was the period in which Romans for the first time wrote long accounts of their own religious tradition – in the work of Varro and his followers, who mapped out the complexities of priesthoods, deities, sacred formulae, and rituals; but it was also the period in which serious intellectual debates took place on religious questions, admittedly questions already set by Greek philosophers. Another is the level of poetry, again under heavy influence from the Greeks, but still bringing Roman concerns directly into public attention. Again, there is the practical level of building and innovating in public space: all the great Roman leaders of the century from Sulla onwards sought to make their mark in part by involvement in great building schemes.[28] In this respect they were fully in the tradition of previous generations, though building on a far more spectacular scale than their ancestors had. In this expansion and restructuring of Rome, temples and other religious monuments played a leading role. To put it at its lowest, a great deal of money, time, and effort was put into religious monuments both before and after the fall of the Republic and the establishment of the new régime.

It would not be an exaggeration to say that the competition between the political leaders of the late Republic – Sulla and Marius, Pompey and Caesar, Mark Antony and Octavian, who was destined to be the victor and take the name Augustus, – was fought out to a significant extent in the language of religion. Their careers were accompanied by omens of success and triumph; they claimed special connections with gods and goddesses and to be blessed by the gods with a special relationship to ensure success. The classic statement is that of Cicero while commenting on the merits of his hero, Pompey, and arguing that he and not his rivals should be given the command of a Roman army in the East:

It remains for me to talk about ⟨Pompey's⟩ *felicitas*, a virtue to be claimed by no man on his own behalf, but only remembered and recorded on another's behalf; even then it must be expressed with caution and conciseness, as is only right and proper when a man speaks of the power of the gods . . .In the case of certain supreme individuals, they have a sort of good fortune divinely implanted in them that brings them greatness, fame, and mighty achievements.   (Cicero, *On the Command of Pompey* 47)

What is to be noted here is not only the significance of the claim that military success is attached to particular individuals by the gods, a claim

---

[28] Gros (1976); Zanker (1988), 104–14; *RoR* i.121–5.

that is barely tolerable in terms of a republican system that depends on the annual rotation of offices; it is also the language in which the claim is expressed, a language of hesitation and reluctance to refer to powers beyond human understanding that might be put at risk by excessive precision or boasting. *Felicitas* is not luck, that might be thought to be determined by chance or accident; it is a gift to specific individuals that the gods might revoke, so that even mentioning it might cause the commander to lose his gift. But the commander with the gift is the one to win the battles.

The narrative of religious history implied here is not therefore a simple story of the decline of a once powerful religious life. Rather, all the evidence suggests that politically active Romans of this period had to reckon with religion and the gods as important factors in determining events and in expressing their claims to authority and command. All the same, there are profound changes in progress; they are not perhaps caused by religious attitudes, but they do find one of their modes of visibility through the competitive religious activities of powerful individuals. The earlier part of this chapter argued that the religion of the Republican period was one expression of the ideology of the ruling élite, of their techniques of sharing power and of limiting the ambitions of the great families. What happens at the end of the Republic is the erosion of the restraints on which this republican system rested.

What follows in the decades after Caesar's murder opens up another problem of interpretation, which can be solved in various ways. What cannot be placed in doubt is that Augustus, the first of the *principes*, the earliest Emperors of Rome, used his new position of sole power very effectively if somewhat cautiously to create exactly the position that had never existed under the Republic. He became himself a member of all the colleges of priests; he also became *pontifex maximus,* though in this case he delayed for reasons of propriety. The *pontifex maximus* at the point when Augustus acquired supreme power was a colleague, who went out of favour with the new régime. Augustus awaited his death before he took the office himself in 12 BC.[29] The great sculptured relief of this period (the *Ara Pacis*) from about this date is probably showing him in the new role of *pontifex maximus* and leading all the other priests in procession.[30] If so, it is encapsulating the new and revolutionary

---

[29] The *Res Gestae* (left to be published after his death) unapologetically lists all his seven priesthoods at ch. 7.3. His version of the delay in becoming *pontifex maximus* and his eventual popular election in 12 BC, at 10.2.

[30] Zanker (1988), 120–5; *RoR* ii.4.3.

religious order of the Imperial period and he was to be followed in holding the office of *pontifex maximus* by all his successors until the fourth century AD. From this point onwards, very little is heard about proceedings in the great colleges, even though we know that they long continued to function and to appoint new members to their number. When points of religious law were to be decided, it was the Emperor, as *pontifex maximus*, who advised the senate.[31]

Even more significant than the formal acquisition of priestly office was the more informal, but unmistakeable, acquisition of all religious initiative. It is quite clear, for instance, how Augustus and his great supporter Marcus Agrippa dominated the holding of the Secular Games in 17 BC.[32] He himself claims responsibility for the restoration of temples and the building of new ones in his account of his own life.[33] It is to him that the restoration of some lost institutions is attributed in the sources: in the case of the priest of Jupiter (the *flamen Dialis*) this is probably right, because although we have no certainty about the exact date of this restoration, it seems likely that he was waiting to be *pontifex maximus* himself before choosing the new *flamen*.[34] The college of the Arval Brethren was put into action far earlier, probably already in 29 BC.[35] The details of some of this may not be very clear, but the general trend seems quite inevitable. Once the holder of the religious power was the same individual as the holder of the political control of the new régime in Rome, he became quite rapidly the head of the state religion and his actions increasingly reflected this position.

One other area shows even more dramatically the direction in which events moved in this period. Two major cults, one of them specially associated with Augustus and the other the most central of all Roman cults, were brought into the closest association with Augustus' own house on the Palatine. The temple of Apollo was built adjacent to it; and a new temple of Vesta was incorporated in it.[36] The reason for this was that that the traditional residence of the *pontifex maximus* was in the forum near to the old temple of Vesta. It is hard to imagine a gesture which sums up the new situation more clearly than this transfer of the religious hearth of Rome into the new house of the emperor-priest.

---

[31] as at Tacitus *Annals* 3.58–9; 71.
[32] Texts *RoR* ii.5.7b.
[33] *Res Gestae* 19–21; 20.4 (the restorations).
[34] For another view, Bowersock (1990).
[35] Scheid (1990), 690–732; *RoR* ii.4.5.
[36] Apollo and Vesta: Zanker (1988), 194–205; 210–15; *RoR* i.189–91; 199–201; *RoR* ii.4.2.

IV. GODS, GODDESSES, AND THEIR TEMPLES

Roman deities are not very easy to classify. They were never organized into a pantheon in ancient Rome, so that we cannot say there was a fixed number of them or that they fulfilled particular functions divided between them. Some of them are clearly part of the Roman tradition from the earliest periods of the city; some are later additions, introduced at specific dates with specific ceremonies, which the Romans carefully recorded. Some have very complicated histories, having multiple associations with different areas of life and often different additional names, defining a particular aspect of the deity. Others seems to exist only because of a particular function or particular moment. Some have special priests, or in the single case of Vesta, priestesses; many, however, do not, but fall within the ambit of the major college of the *pontifices*.

It would be possible for us to invent or construct groups amongst them for our own purposes: we could, for instance, speak of major deities as opposed to minor ones. Of the most important there would be no doubt (Jupiter, Juno, Mars, Apollo), but there would be little agreement as to where the borderline came between the major and the minor ones. There is a distinction between deities that had temples and those that did not, but the former list is constantly increasing as new deities are added and some deities are worshipped in groves or sanctuaries that are not temples. It is never clear whether the building of a temple does in fact represent the recognition of a new deity. The Magna Mater (Cybele), for instance, had no temple in Rome until she was imported with great ceremonial towards the end of the Hannibalic War (207 BC); so it could be said that she joins the list of major deities at just this date and was not a Roman deity before this date.[1] In fact, it is not clear that the Romans would have agreed about this, since according to the poets she played a role in the earliest history of Rome; they may well have regarded her was a Roman goddess who had wrongly been denied honours before the third century BC.[2] On the other hand, when she did arrive they carefully controlled the way in which she was worshipped, because some of the 'exotic' eastern rituals and practices

---

[1] Livy 29.10.4–11.8; 14.5 = *RoR* Iii.2.7a; Ovid, *Fasti* 4.247–348; Bremmer and Horsfall (1987), 105–11; Gruen (1990), 5–33; Beard (1994).
[2] See below, p. 56.

TABLE 3: *Gods and Goddesses*

Latin name	Greek name	Temple from	Area(s)	Festival	Priest/ess
Aesculapius	Asclepius	292 BC	Health		
Apollo	Apollo	431 BC	Health; prophecy	Ludi Apollinares	
Bacchus	Dionysus	As Liber, see Ceres	Wine, ecstasy		
Ceres	Demeter	493 BC (with Liber, Libera)	Corn	Cerialia April 19	*Flamen*; Priestess for Greek cult
Diana	Artemis	490s BC			
Dis Pater	Hades		Underworld	Ludi saeculares	
Fortuna	Tyche	Regal period	Fortune, luck		
Juno	Hera	See Jupiter	State, child-birth		
Jupiter	Zeus	509 BC (with Juno, Minerva)	State, warfare	Ludi Romani, plebeii (?)	*Flamen*
Magna Mater	Cybele	191 BC		Ludi Megalenses	Priestess *Galli*
Mars	Ares	388 BC	War, agriculture	Salian dances	*Flamen*
Mercury	Hermes	495 BC	Commerce		
Minerva	Athena	See Jupiter	Crafts		
Neptune	Poseidon	3rd century	Sea	Neptunalia July 23	
Quirinus		293 BC		Quirinalia Feb 17	*Flamen*
Saturn	Cronus	497 BC		Saturnalia Dec 17 (etc.)	
Venus	Aphrodite	295 BC	Sex		
Vesta	Hestia	Regal period	The hearth	Vestalia June 9	Vestal Virgins
Vulcan	Hephaestus	3rd century	Metal-working	Volcanalia Aug 23	*Flamen*

characteristic of the Cybele-cult evidently struck them as unsuitable for Romans to take part in.[3]

There does in general seem to have been a sharp distinction in Republican times between gods and men, in the sense that worship is not offered to human beings either in their lifetimes or after their death. The Romans did meet the phenomenon of ruler-worship when they had close dealings with Greek cities and eventually they came to accept quasi-divine honours for leading Romans, though it seems to take a century or so before they accepted this.[4] But it is not really until the time of Julius Caesar that the separate categories of humans and gods started to mingle. We have seen above[5] that in the very earliest myths of the city, the founders do already cross the boundary, so there must already have existed a mental template to which the ruler-cult could be fitted. But, as we have also seen, in other respects too the myths of kings provided the Romans with models of how real republican Romans should not behave, rather than how they should.

The interactions of gods and men are constant but almost always through the medium of ritual action. There are few, if any, incidents that we know about in which the gods intervene directly in human affairs by changing events or appearing in a visible form.[6] It would not be right, however, to think of them as being remote from human affairs or more interested in their own business. In some ways, they were very present, not just as statues at home in their temples, but paraded through the streets, sitting at the games that are held in their honour, feasted in public on special occasions. There is a sense in which the gods and goddesses of Rome were citizens belonging to the city just as much as the human citizens and participating in its triumphs and defeats as well as in its rituals.[7] Certainly, all serious actions of the city involved repeated consultations, both through the auspices and through sacrifices; a victory was celebrated by a famous procession, the triumph, in which the army and its general paraded through the city to make sacrifice to Jupiter on the Capitol;[8] and the state defined its relationship

---

[3] For these controls, Dionysius of Halicarnassus, *Roman Antiquities* 2.19 = *RoR* ii.8.7a. The regulations are not dated, but it seems very unlikely that they would have been imposed at any time other than the first arrival of the cult.

[4] The cult of Rome (*dea Roma*) seems to have been introduced instead of ruler-cult: Mellor (1975); Price (1984), 40–43; *RoR* i.158–60.   [5] Above pp. 4–7.

[6] There are very rare exceptions: e.g. the appearance of Castor and Pollux at the battle of Lake Regillus (496 BC), Dionysius of Halicarnassus, *Roman Antiquities* 6.13.1–2, and again at Pydna (168 BC), Cicero, *On the Nature of the Gods* 2.6.

[7] So Scheid (1985), pp. 51–7.

[8] Triumphs: Versnel (1970); Scullard (1981), 213–18; *RoR* ii.5.8.

to the divine citizens by taking regular and extraordinary vows in which they were promised rewards in return for sustained support.[9]

We have texts preserved in Livy's History that provide some idea of the assumptions that lie behind this kind of transaction: the burden of them is to offer games or other ritual actions to the gods in return for protection for the state over a defined period of time.[10] This type of document is often characterized as legalistic and contractual; the Romans certainly do bring to their religious texts the same precision and care with language that characterizes their legal drafting as well; and they evidently did believe that the gods and goddesses could be asked to accept a careful definition of what the state was offering to them and what it was not offering. In the famous vow, taken during the Hannibalic War, which bound the Romans to sacrifice the whole of the new-born offspring of the flocks in a single year, the vow lays down that any kind of ritual procedure would be valid.[11] In a sense this is dictating to the gods; but it is (a) necessary to do this, because in a multiple sacrifice of this kind, it would have been impossible to maintain a common standard of ritual action; and (b) this is not in fact a question of dictating, but of defining the nature of the offer. The vow is not contractual in that it placed no obligation on the gods to accept the offer. Only the Romans were bound to fulfil the terms of the vow, if the gods chose freely to accept the offer. It is all the same revealing that the gods are perceived as thoughtful and rational, to be approached with argument and precision of language. They knew what they were getting, and acted accordingly.

Another regular medium of interchange, as we have already seen, was the prodigy and the handling of prodigies.[12] A prodigy is a reported event in Roman territory, which the Romans accepted as contrary to what they thought of as natural and hence a sign of a major disruption in their relationship with divine powers. This is especially important for our understanding of the religion of Rome, for several reasons, some of them admittedly accidental. One reason is simply that these events and their results are regularly recorded by Livy as part of history; another is that other writers chose to record his lists, so that the prodigy lists sometimes survive even for the periods where Livy's text is missing; we thus have a flow of evidence from the middle Republic to the early Empire and hence a basis for comparison over a relatively long period of

[9] State vows: *RoR* i.32–5.
[10] e.g. Livy 26.2.2–5 (191 BC).
[11] Livy 22.10 = *RoR* ii.6.5; Heurgon (1957).
[12] On prodigies in general: MacBain (1982); Rosenberger (1998).

time.[13] The second reason is that dealing with the prodigies involved in one way or another almost all the groups who had influence on decision-making – the priestly colleges, the senate, the magistrates, even occasionally the Roman people. As we have seen already,[14] these entries provide us with our best information about how these groups co-operated and what roles they played. It is necessary to be very careful in defining what this evidence means so far as the understanding of the gods' role is concerned. It is evident that this was a very important area in the Romans' conception of the relationship of men and women with gods and goddesses; but how are we to interpret their actions?

The simplest, but crudest, option would be to assume a framework of causation and then to attribute the resulting system of belief to the Romans. So we might say that they believed that the gods were angry and were therefore intervening directly in the natural process by sending down monsters or strange forms of rain and hail; that the gods required to be appeased by offerings; and that only when appeased would they restore the balance of nature. We could well say that some thought process of this kind must have underpinned their actions or they would not have made sense at all. But even if so, we still have to recognize that this is not at all the way in which our surviving texts ever speak when they are reporting prodigies. To put it another way, this type of interpretation belongs not to an attempt to understand religious prac-tices, or to imagine the frame of mind in which they might have been undertaken, but to an attack on them by way of reducing them to near absurdity. All religious language risks this kind of abusive reductionism because in order to make statements about the powers that – according to the believers themselves – lie outside and above ordinary life, there is no language to be used except the language of ordinary life, to be understood in symbolic terms.[15] The attacker need only press the literal meaning of the language to produce absurd and indefensible results. The technique works well on prodigies, but it can be used just as effectively against (e.g.) the Christian Eucharist.

The fact is that the sources we have are markedly inexplicit about the nature of the connection between the occurrence of the prodigy, predictions that might be based on it, and the actions (*remedia*) finally

---

[13] The lists derive either from Livy or from Julius Obsequens, whose work preserved the lists from many years where Livy's text itself is lost; between them they provide a steady flow from 218 BC to 43 BC.

[14] See above, pp. 27–9 and Table 2.

[15] See Gordon (1980).

taken to restore the damaged relationship implied by the prodigy itself. We have something like a full text of only one priestly response, but that one does suggest that the ingredients included not just a list of actions to be taken and deities to be placated, but also human offences that might have caused the trouble.[16] If it is typical of others where we do not know all the details, we should recognize a network of human failings, of events seen as exceeding natural limits, and gods needing repayment. This may give us the right way to understand what happened, but we still need to remember how reluctant Roman authors were to pull these elements together into a coherent explanation, and to respect their reluctance.[17]

Another medium through which this contact was mediated was the provision and maintenance of temples. At all dates we know about, the Romans built new temples and maintained the ones they had.[18] This was, therefore, an activity in which a great deal of care and money was invested over a long period of time. In particular, the creation of new sacred sites, whether full-scale temples or sanctuaries with an altar, was a matter of public concern and potential conflict.[19] Many Republican temples resulted from vows taken by generals in battle, who sometimes conducted the placing of contracts and the consecration ceremony themselves; but these were official occasions controlled by priests and senate.[20] It may be that families sought to maintain their prestige by keeping the responsibility for building and maintaining particular temples, though even if the original taker of the vow is remembered, this ongoing connection is not often achieved. In the course of time, the space of Rome the city became transformed by growing numbers of these temples in prominent positions and sometimes grouped within colonnades.[21] They served not just as a visible record of Rome's gradually increasing military dominance over the Mediterranean world but of the contribution to it of new gods and new goddesses at every stage.

[16] This is the response of the *haruspices* to which Cicero's speech, *On the Response of the Haruspices*, is devoted. He quotes it section by section, discussing each as he goes along: for a composite text, *RoR* ii.7.**4a**.

[17] For discussion of the whole issue, see Jason Davies (unpublished dissertation, UCL).

[18] See Table 4, for a selection: full lists (apart from temples to the *Divi*) in Latte (1960), 415–18; Gros (1976); Ziolkowski (1992); Orlin (1997); *RoR* i.87–91; 121–4; 196–201; 253–9; *RoR* ii.**4.1–2**; **7;9**.

[19] Cicero, *On his House* 136, quotes two occasions on which attempted dedications were cancelled by the *pontifices* on the grounds that they had not been approved by act of the people. The conflict over Cicero's house is in the same category.

[20] On the procedure, Orlin (1997).

[21] For such a group, see the temples in the Largo Argentina in Rome, Ziolkowski (1992); Claridge (1998), 215–19.

TABLE 4: *Temple Foundations*

509 BC	Jupiter Optimus Maximus, Juno and Minerva on the Capitoline
495 BC	Mercury near the Circus Maximus
493 BC	Ceres Liber and Libera near the Circus Maximus
	Diana on the Aventine
	Minerva on the Aventine
431 BC	Apollo near the theatre of Marcellus
396 BC	Juno Regina on the Aventine
305 BC	Victoria on the Palatine
292 BC	Aesculapius on the Island
c.292 BC	Hercules Invictus near the Circus
263/2 BC	Minerva on the Aventine
250s BC	Spes (Hope) in the Forum Holitorium
"	Fides (Faith) on the Capitoline
mid-third c. BC	Neptune in the Flaminian Circus
233 BC	Honos (Honour) at the Porta Capena
223 BC	Hercules Magnus Custos in the Flaminian Circus
222 BC	Honos and Virtus (Honour and Virtue)
215 BC	Venus of Eryx on the Capitoline
194 BC	Juno Sospita in the Forum Holitorium
191 BC	Magna Mater on the Palatine
191 BC	Hercules of the Muses in the Flaminian Circus
181 BC	Pietas (Piety) in the Forum Holitorium
146 BC	Felicitas (Felicity) in the Velabrum
138 BC	Mars in the Campus
101 BC	Fortuna huiusce diei (the Fortune of this day) in the Campus
55 BC	Venus Victrix, Honos, Virtus, Felicitas in the marble theatre
29 BC	Divus Julius in the Forum Romanum
28 BC	Apollo on the Palatine
2 BC	Mars Ultor in the Forum of Augustus
After AD14	Divus Augustus on the Palatine
Caligula (?)	Isis and Sarapis in the Campus Martius
Vespasian	Divus Claudius on the Caelian
AD 75	Pax in the Forum of Pax
AD 128	Venus and Roma on the Via Sacra
Hadrian	Divus Trajanus in the Forum of Trajan

As often, we can only assess the importance of a particular activity when it comes to attention in a crisis. In the case of temples, we have good reason to think that the state normally took some care to see that they did not fall into a state of decline or disrepair. It is only in the civil war period, when government seemed to have collapsed and repeated warfare broke out between the armies of Rome, that the repair of temples becomes what we should call a headline issue. According a famous ode of Horace:

> However innocent a Roman yourself, you will pay the penalty for your fathers' failures, until you have restored the collapsing temples and the images foul with black filth. You hold power because you recognize yourself as lesser than the gods: that is the starting-point and that will be the end-point. Neglected gods have visited many a trouble on the grieving West.   (Horace, *Odes* 3.6)

In other words, the neglected gods are marked by the neglected temples and the restoration of them becomes a prime objective of reconstruction after the war. If Horace sets out the programme of action, Augustus' own account of his activities in his *Res Gestae* tells us how he thought he had dealt with the matter:

> I restored eighty-two temples of the gods within the city ⟨of Rome⟩ as consul for the sixth time ⟨28 BC⟩ on the authority of the senate, not passing over any that needed restoration at the time.   (*RG* 20.4)

There is room for some scepticism here about Augustus' claims and their significance: if he could restore so many temples in a single year, he cannot have been making any fundamental changes or reconstruction. It is hard to think that much more can have happened than a lick of paint on the walls. What actually happened, however, matters a great deal less than what was thought to have happened.

The period of Augustus' principate also saw major temple-building in the Republican tradition, though always with reference to his own achievements and the deities to which he was thought to owe those achievements. The most spectacular was probably the temple of Mars Ultor (Mars the Avenger), which was built as the dominating element of his new Forum.[22] It was vowed at the Battle of Philippi in 42 BC, when Augustus (Octavianus, as he was called at the time) defeated his father's murderers – hence the Avenger. Mars was of course also the father of Romulus and Remus, themselves among the ancestors of the Julii. Meanwhile another magnficent temple was built in the 20s BC for

---

[22] Mars: *RoR* ii.4.2.

Apollo, next to Augustus' own house on the Palatine.[23] Apollo too was one of Augustus' specially protective gods and responsible for his victory over Sextus Pompey in 38 BC.[24]

If Augustus was in the tradition of the great Republican temple-builders, his successors did not characteristically follow this example. Temple-building in Rome came to be increasingly devoted to the temples of the new gods, that is the successive dead Emperors, declared as *Divi* after their deaths. The precedent was set, as so often, by Augustus himself, who built the temple to his adoptive father, Divus Julius, in the Roman forum, more or less where the great Roman crowd had built him a funeral pyre in March 44 BC, immediately after the assassination.[25] It was almost sixty years later that Augustus himself was deified on the authority of his successor Tiberius and the Senate of the time and his temple built above the forum.[26] From then onwards almost all the *Divi* received their temples until the time of Marcus Aurelius. Some of these were gigantic buildings, which must have dominated their regions of the city.[27] The old gods were not forgotten and their temples were maintained, but many of the foundations that were not dedicated to Emperors were introducing new deities from abroad or innovating in other ways.[28] There is no question that the Roman tradition of constant innovation and experiment was maintained. The scale and magnificence of the new temples expressed the grandeur of the imperial capital, but the old openness and capacity to innovate can still be seen in such buildings as the Pantheon – which still survives as rebuilt by Hadrian – or the biggest temple of all, dedicated to Venus and Roma, which was innovative both in its structure and in the idea of worshipping the goddess Roma in Rome itself.[29]

[23] Above p. 34.
[24] *RoR* i.198–9.
[25] Weinstock (1971), 385–401.
[26] Tacitus, *Annals* 1.9–10; Steinby (1993–) i.145–6; *RoR* i.208–9.
[27] Steinby (1993–), i.277–8; ii.348–56; *RoR* i.253.
[28] The most visible foreign cult was dedicated to Isis and Sarapis in the Campus Martius. Steinby (1993–), iii.107–9; *RoR* i.264–5.
[29] Claridge (1998), 113–15; 201–7; *RoR* i.257–8.

V. RITUALS

Nobody can doubt that rituals of various kinds were a crucial part of the interactions between men and women and gods and goddesses in the religion of Rome. Rituals marked all public events and celebrations: some of these we would classify as religious occasions – annual festivals, the taking and fulfilling of vows, the anniversaries of temple foundations; others as secular – elections, the assembly of legions for warfare, the census of Roman citizens; still others challenge our own criteria – the games, or dramatic performances, which certainly had ritual elements in the programme, even though we are inclined to regard entertainment as their primary purpose.[1] It is important to see that these are our problems of interpretation: we have no reason to believe that the Romans made such distinctions or found the existence of different types of ritual in itself problematic.

Far more difficult for us is the fact that, although they wrote about rituals in the sense of referring to them by name and describing what was done – particularly if something was done wrong so that the ritual went amiss or had to be repeated – the expounding of rituals was not often done at all. So, for instance, there is no doubt that the central ritual of the religious life of the Romans was animal sacrifice. Yet we have virtually no discussions of what it signified and only two substantial accounts of it, one from Dionysius of Halicarnassus, whose purpose was to prove that the Romans were really Greeks, and therefore compares Roman practices to Greek;[2] the other from a Christian writer whose interest was mainly to mock at the practice of pagans, but who does at least try to discuss the significance of what was done.[3] With these two exceptions we have massive evidence of practice to consider, but almost no statement of theory.

We can see that the ritual programme was complex and highly articulated; and we can infer at least some of the principles on which it worked. Two points are very clear: first, that the sacrifice was bound closely by rules and traditions that had to be followed; secondly, that the skill of the sacrificers allowed communication between men and gods, which at least guaranteed that the worshippers could have confidence in

---

[1] Hopkins (1991).

[2] Dionysius of Halicarnassus, *Roman Antiquities* 7.72.15–18.

[3] Arnobius, *Against the Gentiles* 7, on whom see Liebeschuetz (1979), 254–60.

the outcome of the actions. The victims had to be in perfect condition; their species, colour, age, and sex had to be appropriate to the deity concerned; in almost all cases the victims were domestic animals, not wild ones – mostly sheep, cattle, goats, and pigs. They were decorated and brought in procession to the altar to which they had to come placidly, as willing offerings to the deity.[4] There then followed the placing of meal and wine on the victim's head (the action called *immolatio*) and a prayer in which the god or goddess had to be named. The actual killing had to be instantaneous and obviously required high skill from the assistants. Another skilled official, the *haruspex*, examined the entrails to see that they were as they should be.[5] The victim could now be butchered, the cuts divided between those returned to the gods and those destined for human consumption; finally, the meat was cooked and eaten by the worshippers at a feast at the end of the day. Surplus meat could evidently be sold in the market.[6]

It was quite essential that this should all be carried out without hitches or mistakes. It could happen that the victim escaped, a highly inauspicious event; or the *haruspex* might find disease or malformation in the entrails, or an organ missing.[7] Any such irregularity had to lead to repetition of the sacrifice, until a successful outcome (*litatio*) was reached. Failure to reach such a successful completion of the ritual was an irremediably bad sign for any planned undertaking. It is not difficult to see the value of this from a functional point of view: once a successful outcome had been reached and announced, although that did not offer any guarantee of success, it did afford one of the preconditions for success. We can just occasionally see, through sources mostly interested in Roman victories, the disastrous effect on morale once the idea had become established that the generals could not obtain the right results in sacrificing before a campaign.[8]

There are many other rituals that are less central, sometimes less well attested than sacrifice: the taking of the auspices before any action; the taking of vows before or during action; the various ritual remedies (*remedia*) that averted the evil consequences of prodigies; rituals and

---

[4] For these stages: Warde Fowler (1911), 179–91; *RoR* ii.148–50 (including some visual evidence, on which see further Ryberg (1955)).

[5] *RoR* i.36; ii.**7.4b & d.**

[6] I Corinthians 8.10; Pliny, Letters 10.96.10= *RoR* ii.**11.11b**.

[7] For a missing heart, see Cicero, *On Divination* 1.119.

[8] For an occasion on which the sacrifice went wrong and never was successfully completed, see Livy 41.14.7 and 15.1–4 = *RoR* ii.**7.4c**.

processions of celebration or of mourning and so on. The great festivals of the Roman year are known to us through one of the most valuable documents we have of Republican religion, that is the ritual calendar. Many copies of this survive, almost all of them dating from the time of Augustus, and they are found in many towns of Italy.[9] The calendars vary in the amount of detail they give, but they contain as their common core a series of festivals marked in capital letters and these include many of the most famous. For the first half of the year, we also have a learned and witty commentary on the festivals in the form of Ovid's poem, *The Fasti*. Occasionally too, one or other of the festivals is mentioned for one reason or another in our general historical sources. But it has to be recognized that much of the detail of the annual programme is quite obscure to us and that some of it was even obscure already to the Romans themselves.[10]

In the inscribed copies of the calendar certain festivals are entered in capital letters and it seems certain that this list of capital-letter festivals must have some special meaning; it includes some of the most famous festivals of Rome, but also omits some of the major deities and includes some very minor ones.[11] In smaller letters are religious occasions that were created in the Republican period, such as the various sets of games, many of which were created at recorded dates, and the anniversary festivals of temples, again well-dated Republican events.[12] A great deal of scholarly work has been put into the attempt to explain these ancient festivals partly by studying the evidence about them, partly by looking for parallels in other times and places; but much of this work has rested on the assumption that by understanding the origin of the festival, its inner meaning will become clear: so that it can be classified as a festival of purification, or of fertility, or of initiation of the young or whatever. It may now be suspected that this was a wrong approach. Neither the accounts of the ritual nor the myths and stories attached them ever make the question of origins clear (if it ever can be clear) and meanwhile the evidence does imply strongly that the significance of different festivals

---

[9] Wallace-Hadrill (1987). For a discussion of the individual festivals Scullard (1981), useful as a collection of evidence but not to be trusted in its interpretations. For the month of April, *RoR* ii.60–77.

[10] Varro, *On the Latin Language* 6.19, says that the name of Furrina, who had a festival in her honour (25th July), was almost unknown in his day.

[11] See the list of festivals Table 5; omitted from the capital-letter list are some major deities (Jupiter, Mars, Juno and many others); but they do often receive honours at festivals not dedicated to them as Jupiter at the Vinalia (23rd April) or Mars at the Equus October (the October Horse) (15th October).

[12] The distinction is clear from the reproduction of the calendar from Antium under *RoR* ii.3.2.

changed quite dramatically over long periods of time.[13] This is, after all, only what might be expected: there were no explanations or even myths attached to many occasions, only sequences of ritual actions and prayers. It seems only too likely that the interpretations placed on these actions would not remain static, but shift with shifting ideas and situations.

One festival will provide an example of this multiplicity of meanings. The Lupercalia was celebrated on February 15. We have information about the festival from early times (we know at least that it was one of the capital letter festivals in the old calendars), through references coming from the late Republican antiquarians, down to a discussion by Gelasius, bishop of Rome in the fifth century AD, who defended his decision to forbid Christians from taking part in the ritual, which was evidently going strong though perhaps in a modified form.[14] But the existence of a number of mentions over a long period of time does not provide us with any certain clue to the meaning of the festival. One of its most striking components was the running of the Luperci, the priests responsible for the festival, almost naked through the streets of Rome, striking the women they met with whips of goatskin; the women accepted the blows in the hope that these would encourage pregnancy.[15] But should this be seen as the central significance of the rite, or just an associated 'superstition'? For Julius Caesar and his supporters in the 40s BC, it seems clear that the ritual was read not as a fertility ritual, but rather as a coronation, because they selected it as a suitable moment at which to try the offering of a crown to Caesar by one of the Luperci, while in the middle of performing his ritual run.[16] Nor can this association be an accident, because there is a strong tradition associating the festival with the first King of Rome, Romulus, and his twin, Remus. They are represented as the prototype of the runners, when they compete to be the first to protect the flocks of the new settlement from bandits.[17] The importance of goats in the ritual programme also supports the association with pastoralism and hence with the founders, who are always represented as herdsmen.[18] It is, however, anything but clear that the ritual developed as an expression of the Romulus myth:

[13] Beard (1987).
[14] For Gelasius: Holleman (1974); Hopkins (1991); *RoR* ii.5.2e.
[15] Ovid, *Fasti* 2.425–52.
[16] Weinstock (1971), 331–40; *RoR* ii.5.2b.
[17] Wiseman (1995), 77–88. Though it is surprising and not satisfactorily explained that the winner in this race should be Remus, not Romulus.
[18] Ampolo (1988).

TABLE 5: *The main festivals of the Roman Calendar*

January	1	KAL(endae)
	5	NON(ae)
	9	AGONALIA
	11	CARMENTALIA
	13	EID(us)
	15	CARMENTALIA
February	1	KAL(endae)
	5	NON(ae)
	13	EID(us)
	15	LUPERCALIA
	17	QUIRINALIA
	21	FERALIA
	23	TERMINALIA
	24	REGIFUGIUM
	27	EQUIRRIA
March	1	KAL(endae)
	7	NON(ae)
	14	EQUIRRIA
	15	EID(us)
	17	LIBERALIA. AGONALIA
	23	TUBILUSTRIUM
April	1	KAL(endae)
	5	NON(ae)
	13	EID(us)
	15	FORDICIDIA
	19	CERIALIA
	21	PARILIA
	23	VINALIA
	25	ROBIGALIA
May	1	KAL(endae)
	7	NON(ae)
	9	LEMURIA
	11	LEMURIA
	13	LEMURIA
	15	EID(us)
	21	AGONALIA
	23	TUBILUSTRIUM
June	1	KAL(endae)
	5	NON(ae)
	9	VESTALIA
	11	MATRALIA
	13	EID(us)

TABLE 5 (*cont.*):

July	1	KAL(endae)
	5	POPLIFUGIA
	7	NON(ae)
	15	EID(us)
	19	LUCARIA
	21	LUCARIA
	23	NEPTUNALIA
	25	FURRINALIA
August	1	KAL(endae)
	7	NON(ae)
	13	EID(us)
	17	PORTUNALIA
	19	VINALIA
	21	CONSUALIA
	23	VOLCANALIA
	25	OPICONSIVIA
	27	VOLTURNALIA
September	1	KAL(endae)
	5	NON(ae)
	13	EID(us)
October	1	KAL(endae)
	7	NON(ae)
	11	MEDITRINALIA
	13	FONTINALIA
	15	EID(us)
	19	ARMILUSTRIUM
November	1	KAL(endae)
	5	NON(ae)
	13	EID(us)
December	1	KAL(endae)
	5	NON(ae)
	11	AGONALIA
	13	EID(us)
	15	CONSUALIA
	17	SATURNALIA
	19	OPALIA
	21	DIVALIA
	23	LARENTALIA

many details of the myth do not fit well with the ritual, though it seems likely enough that each will have influenced the other.

There are other elements as well in the accounts we have. Some sources seem to imply that the running of the Luperci was circular and therefore that its purpose was the purification or protection of the ancient settlement.[19] The word Lupercus might be associated with wolves or the protection of the community from wolves.[20] Other sources speak not of running round, but of running up and down, on the site of the later *forum*, which we know in early times was a burying ground. It is not in fact even clear whether the Luperci did follow a fixed route, though it is quite likely that they did. Varro, the great antiquarian of late Republican Rome, (who seems to support one of these two routes in one passage, the other in another passage), strongly associates the whole ritual with purification and speaks of this as the period of the gods of the underworld and the dead. This creates yet another possible interpretation.[21]

Some points stand out here. For instance, that there is no reason for us to insist that some of these interpretations were wrong and some of them right. They come from different authorities at different periods and the reasonable assumption is that they are all in some sense right. For some of our informants (especially Ovid[22] and Plutarch[23]), the purpose of their accounts seems precisely to be to parade the multiplicity of views about the rituals, as a way of demonstrating their learning and the importance of the theme about which they are writing. We could say that this parade of interpretations would also have been one of the component experiences of those who attended the festivals. On this view, we should be thinking not that if we only knew the ritual better, our doubts would be resolved for us; but rather that the more we knew of the ritual, the more clearly we would see that there was no single answer to its interpretation, that every participant would have had his or her own idea of what it all meant.

This is the clearest example of the multiple explanation of a festival that we have; but it is also the festival about which we have the greatest volume of information and discussion. On some other festivals we have little or nothing to give us clues as to their significance, let alone their

---

[19] For the route: *RoR* ii.5.2d.
[20] For this view: Plutarch, *Life of Romulus* 21.
[21] Purification: Varro, *On the Latin Language* 6.34.
[22] *Fasti* 2.267–452; see Feeney (1998), 120; 132.
[23] Above n. 20.

development over time; but evidently the standing of the different festivals varied widely, some being universally known, some virtually lost in oblivion. Nor is this surprising. For one thing, it is in this respect very much like modern religious calendars, which also have one or two festivals of wide fame (Christmas, Easter) and plenty of others of great obscurity to all but the very committed (Septuagesima Sunday, Rogationtide). Secondly, as we have seen already, the pattern of much pagan development would have consisted of forgetting and replacing, and the calendar would have been no exception to this. Since we know of many accretions, we should expect to find losses as well. The accretions consist, for instance, of all the many sets of games (*ludi*) that had been added by the end of the Republican period.

Another respect in which the festivals vary widely from one another is in terms of their impact on the community. Some of them seem to have consisted entirely of ritual action by the priests, Vestals, or officials; but others involve a great deal of activity in families, or in the countryside, or by the whole population. The festivals in honour of the dead take place in a family context, whether in the house or at the tombs of ancestors;[24] the Saturnalia festival was celebrated in the house, where role-swapping and gift exchange, among other things, took place;[25] we have of course no way of knowing how universal these practices were, but no reason to doubt that they were widely observed. It is only in the very late Republic that the population of Rome became so huge, and in some ways so short-term, that it is hard to see how knowledge of the festivals can have been a binding factor in the city's life, let alone of all the citizens of Rome, now spread over the whole of Italy.[26] In earlier periods, we have every reason to think that these would have been essentially Roman annual events and that knowledge of them would have been part of the essential education for anyone who regarded him- or herself as a Roman. That is no doubt why copies of the Calendar were so widely disseminated through Roman Italy in the Augustan period.

There is no question at all that one category of festival did attract mass interest. The games (*ludi*) probably go back to the earliest times of Rome, though only two sets, the *ludi plebeii* and the *ludi Romani* were established in the early Republic; but other sets and more days were

---

[24] Scullard (1981), 74–6 (13–22 February).

[25] Scullard (1981), 205–7 (17–23 December).

[26] The population of Rome is generally agreed to have reached one million by the time of Augustus. Much of this population must represent a constant flow of immigration from the countryside, and freed slaves.

added progressively during the late Republic; the number of days given over to the various sets had reached more than fifty by the late Republic, and eventually three times as many in the late Empire.[27] The Games included quite a wide range of competitions and entertainments: there were various forms of racing, dramatic performances, and mime; and displays of wild animals and gladiator fighting. A number of plays still survive that were performed at the Games from the mid-third century BC onwards.[28] Nobody can doubt that their popularity and the multi-plication of days devoted to them were the result of the appeal of the entertainments staged and of the racing, especially chariot-racing, that was on offer. On the other hand, the Games never lost their ritual aspect: the gods and goddesses came down from their temples to watch and there were set religious rituals that had to be performed, indeed performed perfectly, if the ceremony was to be successful.[29] There was also a special college of priests, created in 196 BC, whose duty was the oversight of the games and the religious ceremonies associated with them.[30]

It is also worth noticing that the association between the temple and some form of public performance must have gone back well into the Roman past, because various Italian temples have a theatre attached to them and facing them.[31] This architectural form seems to reflect the fact that early performances happened in a temporary theatre built of wood for a particular occasion.[32] No doubt the god or goddess then appeared on the steps in front of his or her own temple to watch the performance. There was in fact prolonged resistance in Rome to the idea of a permanent, stone-built theatre; and when Pompey in 55 BC finally succeeded in having the first one completed, the new theatre incorpo-rated a temple dedicated to Venus Victrix; thus still respecting the traditional association of theatre and temple.[33]

New rituals as well as new meanings were generated in Imperial as well as Republican times. The innovation perhaps best known to us is the apotheosis ritual of which we have three accounts, varying in detail, but all following the same lines. The ritual was developed from the

---

[27] *RoR* i.263.

[28] *Ludi*: Scullard (1981), 183–6; Bernstein (1998); *RoR* i.66–7; 100–1.

[29] They had to be repeated if there was the slightest error: Cicero, *On the Response of the Haruspices* 23; Bernstein (1998), 84–95.

[30] The *epulones*, see Table 1; their creation *MRR* i.336; 338 (196 BC).

[31] Hanson (1959).

[32] Wooden theatres: Bernstein (1998), 301–3; at the Secular Games, *RoR* ii.5.7b.

[33] For Pompey's theatre: Hanson (1959), 43–55; Weinstock (1971), 80–7; *RoR* i.122–3.

funeral ritual of aristocratic families.[34] There was a procession of famous Romans of the past, representations of the nations of the empire, the guilds of different trades, the senators, and leading members of the order of the *equites*. A speech was made in honour of the dead Emperor, whose body or image was on a bier lying in state. Then the whole assembly processed followed by the bier to a pyre, elaborately decorated. There the bier was placed on the pyre and intricate manoeuvres, in and out of the pyre, were performed by the magistrates, the *equites*, and the troops.[35] Finally fire was set to the pyre and, as the flames mounted up, an eagle was seen to fly from the pyre into the sky, symbolizing the Emperor's ascent to the heavens. The most obvious functions of this programme were to mourn the passing of the Emperor and to display to the leading members of the community, carefully organized by their ranks, the succession of the new Emperor, who had a leading part in the ritual and bade his predecessor farewell. It also works as a confirmation of the new status of the dead man, raised to the level of the gods. But of course, as ever, the means of dealing with the dead have immediate implications for the living. By supervising the deification of his predecessor, the new Emperor was confirming his own rightful role and emphasizing his own piety. The building of a great temple to the new *Divus*, common as we have seen throughout the first and second centuries AD, made his position even more evident in stone and marble.[36] No doubt, this explains for instance why Nero should have started to construct so impressive a monument to a predecessor for whom he had at best limited respect.

It would be possible to proliferate examples of ritual innovations in all periods of Roman history. We shall return later to the significance of this activity in a pagan context.

[34] Price (1987).
[35] *RoR* ii.**9.3b**.
[36] For the temples of the *Divi*, see above, p. 43.

VI. INNOVATION AND ITS ACCOMMODATION

The Sibylline Books played a very central but elusive role in the religious history of the Roman people. Originally, according to the tradition, they consisted of a set of Greek oracles kept by the Romans as one of their holiest texts. The story ran that an old woman offered nine books to King Tarquin (the fifth king, conventionally 616–579 BC) and asked for a price. He refused to buy them at her price; she reacted by destroying three of them and offering the remaining six at the same price; he refused again and she reacted in the same way again, offering the last three for the same price as before. At this point, he was impressed, consulted the priests, and at last realized his mistake, thus agreeing to buy the last three books at her original price.[1]

Later on at least, the books were attributed to the Sibyl, a wise ancient woman who received her inspiration from Apollo. Ancient tradition knew of several different Sibyls, identified by their different geographic locations all over the Mediterranean world and also further East.[2] The Roman Books were supposed to have come from the Italian Sibyl, who supposedly dwelt in a cave at Cumae. The Romans and Etruscans of the sixth century BC were certainly in close contact with the Greeks living in Campania and South Italy, so there is nothing impossible about the arrival of Greek prophetic texts at this time. It is less certain whether the connection with the Cumaean Sibyl is original (she is not named in the versions of the story that survive) or whether that is a later explanation of the Books being in Greek verse. It seems significant that this new text is connected in the mythical tradition with Tarquin, a king from abroad himself, said to have been a Greek from Corinth, and not with Romulus or Numa.[3] From this point on the Romans claim to have had a special college of priests, called 'the two men for sacrifices' (*duoviri sacris faciundis*), who, as discussed earlier in this book, advised the senate on the contents of the Books, in the case of dreadful prodigies or disasters.[4]

In a more general sense too, this college seems to have been made responsible for the .control of Greek cults in Roman life. Under the

---

[1] For the story, Dionysius of Halicarnassus, *Roman Antiquities*, 4.62 = *RoR* ii.1.8.
[2] Parke (1988).
[3] For the origins of Tarquin, *Oxford Classical Dictionary* (1996[3]), 1475.
[4] For this college, see above, p. 25 and Table 1.

Empire, we sometimes find documents that show them playing this part, amongst communities of Roman citizens in other parts of Italy:

> The *quindecimviri sacris faciundis* greet the *praetores* and the other magistrates of Cumae. We hear from your letter that you have created Licinius Secundus priest of the Mother of the Gods in the place of the late Claudius Restitutus. At your request, we authorize him to wear the armlet and the crown, but only within your colony.[5]

This control over foreign imported cults must go back to Republican Rome and was evidently associated with the control of the Greek Books. The Romans do in fact have a set of cults which are celebrated by what they called the 'Greek rite' (*Graeco ritu*); the most obvious rule was that you conducted the sacrifice with your head uncovered, unlike the 'Roman rite' in which you drew your toga over your head.[6] Whether these procedures were really Greek does not matter; but it is characteristic of the Romans that they carefully preserved the different ceremonies and saw some rituals as native, some foreign, yet both part of their own tradition.[7]

Many of the cults in which the Greek rite was used were those introduced by the Sibylline Books on the recommendation of the college. Notable examples of this are: Ceres, Liber and Libera (496 BC), Aesculapius (293 BC), Venus of Eryx (217 BC), all of them having close connections to Greek cults from different areas.[8] The Sibylline Books are not the only medium through which changes, modifications, and additions to the religion of the Romans could take place. It was possible for a commander to vow a temple to a new deity in the course of his command. If he was victorious, then on his return, he would still need the support of the priests, the senate, and the people to carry out his vow, but many new temples originated in this way.[9] One celebrated innovation in the course of the Hannibalic War arose from a prophetic text, but explicitly not one of those in the Sibylline collection – indeed the text was apparently local, written in Latin and only discovered when prophetic texts were confiscated by the magistrates as a measure of control. Parts of it may be preserved in Livy's text.[10] In other

---

[5] *ILS* 4175 = *RoR* ii.**10.4b**. The date is AD 289 and the section quoted is preceded by a decree of the local authorities in Cumae, which must have been sent to the college for its approval.

[6] For the Greek rite, Gagé (1955); *RoR* i.70–1, 173–4; *RoR* ii.7.5a, 7.5c.

[7] Discussion in Scheid (1996).

[8] For the three cults, see *RoR* i.64–6; 69–70; 83. See Table 4 for the dates at which these temples were completed and dedicated.

[9] Vows: Ziolkowski (1992), 193–261; Orlin (1997).

[10] Livy 25.12.1–13 = *RoR* ii.**7.5c**.

cases again, we simply do not know or cannot trust the information we happen to have available.

There is an apparently serious paradox here. We have clear evidence that a major characteristic of the religious atmosphere was an openness to innovation and adjustment at almost all periods about which we have any worthwhile information at all. There are even regular mechanisms that facilitate and regulate this openness, though it not easy to believe that the Romans would have seen them so explicitly in that light themselves. At the same time, all we know about Roman attitudes shows them clinging at the conscious level to a tradition of the deepest conservatism, valuing the traditions of the past and the ways of their ancestors, and believing that only the most sedulous retention of past practices and rituals can be expected to keep the gods and goddesses active and on their side.

A large part of the explanation must be that much of what we classify as innovation would not have been so perceived by contemporaries. The role of the Sibylline Books themselves, for example, would have been to guarantee that any recommended cult or practice was not in a true sense 'new' at all; but rather a belated recognition of a power that should have been the recipient of worship all along. In one or two cases we have a more substantial picture of what this perceived continuity might have meant. The Magna Mater cult provides a good example – as so often: the cult is in many ways a dramatic innovation, but the title and the location of the new temple give away the fact that she was not seen as a new, strange goddess, but rather as the Mother from Mount Ida, which is the mountain near to Troy.[11] It was to Ida that Aeneas first fled when Troy was destroyed and from there that he began the wanderings that were eventually to lead him to Latium and then his son to the foundation of Alba Longa, the predecessor of Rome. So if the cult was in one sense new, in another it made contact with the profoundest roots of Roman identity.

The Secular Games of the Augustan period provide a very challenging example of this process of repetition and innovation in action. They were a major event involving the whole city and organized by the most senior members of the ruling régime – Augustus himself and his right-hand man Marcus Agrippa.[12] They were presented as part of a sequence

---

[11] Her official title was *Mater Deum Magna Idaea* (Great Mother of the Gods, from Mount Ida); for the mythical connection with Ida, see Ovid, *Fasti* 4.247–72; for discussion, Wiseman (1984); Gruen (1990), 15–19.

[12] See above p. 34.

of such secular celebrations, which had to take place only once in about a century. The date at which Augustus needed to have them held, in order to mark the beginning of a new and better age for mankind, did not fit the established sequence, so a new sequence had to be found, with some creative re-conceiving of history to fit. Far more startling than this, however, is the fact that the rituals themselves were fundamentally changed from the Republican version. Little is clear from the very patchy accounts we have of these earlier events; but we do know that the recipients of the ritual were underworld deities – primarily Dis Pater and his queen, Proserpina. In the Augustan version these have virtually disappeared, to be replaced by Jupiter, Juno, Apollo, and Diana; the ode (the *carmen saeculare*) was written for the occasion by Horace and the text, which survives amongst his other poetry, shows how the whole emphasis must have been transformed from any precedents they had.[13] But it would be far too simple to suggest that this was any kind of deception. For one thing we can detect some elements of continuity in the rituals and prayers, with some formulae and traditions that must have gone back to the earliest celebrations.[14] For another, we can find some of the transitional rituals from the Sibylline tradition that must have contributed to the programme of 17 BC: for instance, the choirs that are a feature of the Secular Games find precedents in other rituals recommended by the Books. Here again the production of an oracle must have been the key event that enabled modification to take place without its being recognized as such by the participants, even if the organizers knew that they were combining different strands of ritual.

If part of the story of religion in Rome consists of a negotiation between change and the accommodation of change, the other side of the coin should not be neglected. If new elements constantly arrive, old ones are just as constantly omitted or forgotten; this process is far harder for us to track, because if new arrivals are at least erratically documented in our sources, losses are never recorded; indeed, given the nature of the ceremonies, many small changes would never have been noticed at all, perhaps not even by the priests at the time. Such changes as they did notice at the time, they had no reason to record and every reason to omit to record, unless they wanted to have them restored. Whether evidenced or not, however, we have to assume that there would always have been

---

[13] See on this Feeney (1998), 32–8; though it should not be forgotten that the hymn was performed within a section of the ritual addressed to Apollo and Diana, so the significance of the emphasis on them should not be pressed too far.
[14] Palmer (1974), 94–108.

an unceasing flux – of old rites into oblivion and of new ones into practice. Even if this state of affairs can all only be inferred not proved, we can find two indirect reflections of it in the later years of the Republican system.

First, at intervals we find the phenomenon of the revival of lost practices. One episode of this seems to have happened at the point in the 140s and 130s BC where we first hear of antiquarian writing in Rome; a series of revivals of antique practices seems to follow, the most notorious being the use of an ancient fetial ritual in the interests of renouncing a treaty made by a defeated general.[15] The general was handed back to the Spanish enemy, naked and bound, as an act of renunciation. More famously still Augustus, when he obtained sole power in Rome, evidently claimed great credit for renewing or restoring various buildings, rituals, and priesthoods that he claimed had been forgotten in the late Republican years and during the years of civil war.[16] This so-called Augustan revival has at times been connected with the theory of terminal 'decline' in the religion of the whole society, so he becomes the restorer of the whole crumbling edifice. It seems fairer to see him as acting very much as many others had before him, almost as a regular part of the cycle of religious life.

It is evidently in close connection with such episodes of revivalism and especially that of the Augustan period, that claims are made by observers that the traditions of the ancestors are being lost and abandoned. This seems to have been a leading theme in Varro's great antiquarian works on Roman religion, from which a good deal of our information ultimately derives. He and Cicero both blame the negligence of the ruling class for this loss of traditional rites and activities.[17] It is hard to resist the idea that what he was doing was drawing attention to a state of affairs that could in theory have been detected at many other dates, but regarding it as evidence of a serious decline. It was only after the civil wars of the 40s and 30s BC that this claim came into its own, providing as it did not only an explanation of what had gone wrong (the gods had been abandoned), but a remedy for the evils of Rome.

The most famous case in point is the failure to fill the office of the *flamen Dialis* after the death of the last holder of the priesthood in 86 BC. It is not clear what the circumstances were in which this would have

---

[15] For the revivals in general: *RoR* i.108–13; for the fetial ritual, Cicero, *On Duties* 3.109; Rosenstein (1990), 136–7; 148–50.

[16] Augustan 'revival' of religion: Warde Fowler (1911), 428–51; *RoR* i.167–210.

[17] For discussion: *RoR* i.125–34; North (1986).

happened; but we do know that a successor was nominated, though apparently never inaugurated. Augustus, perhaps surprisingly, did not have the position filled as soon as he was established in power in the 20s BC, so that the gap in the office lasted in the end for over seventy years. On the other hand, as soon as he became *pontifex maximus*, which he did after the death of his sometime colleague Aemilius Lepidus in 12 BC, he did have a new priest inaugurated and it seems to be this event among others that the great frieze of the Ara Pacis was designed to celebrate, by showing Augustus in the lead and the four *flamines* following behind him.[18] The message is that the damage done by this lapse has at last been healed by the new *pontifex maximus*. To put it into other words we have to recognize that for the proponents of the new Augustan régime, the idea of the past decline of religion was appealing precisely because it supplied tangible, achievable objectives: restore the priesthoods, re-perform the forgotten rituals, clean up the temples: the gods will be appeased and all will come right again.

If for contemporaries this was an opportunity not to be missed, it is this perception of Republican religion that has dramatically misled much modern discussion. From the earliest published work on the subject in the early nineteenth century, it has been an unexamined assumption that the religion of Cicero's age was debased if not extinct, and opinion has only differed as to whether the 'Augustan revival' was a success or always doomed to failure. Only in the last third of the twentieth century has the issue been re-opened and different interpretations of the whole situation offered. What is more, one of the major innovations of the early principate has still further strengthened the modern impression of a religion in terminal decay and, once again, a revision of this outlook is one of the trends in recent debate. The issue this time is the development of ruler cult in the late Republic and early Empire. Both the character of this cult and the history of its development have proved to be highly controversial matters. Some have believed in a new religious force called 'the Imperial cult', created from the start of the Empire and becoming almost a new religion in the course of the first century AD. This notion needs to be treated with some scepticism. First, there is no sign that the cult was organized, still less imposed, from the centre of the empire;[19] there was a good deal of local variation in practice and much

---

[18] On the lapse of the office: *RoR* i.130–2; on the Ara Pacis: Torelli (1982), 27–61, esp 43–4; Elsner (1991); (1995); *RoR* ii.4.3. See above ch. III n. 30.

[19] Bickerman (1973); Price (1984); *RoR* I.206–10.

seems to grow up by local initiative, with or without central consent. Secondly, it is a mistake to overemphasize how new or controversial the innovations were in this regard: in many areas ruler worship seems to have been accepted quite uncritically and to have fitted into existing traditions and assumptions. It is tempting to say that the worship of the Emperor has been more of a problem for modern interpreters than it ever was for ancient worshippers.

Some areas of difficulty there evidently were. For instance, the Jews and the Christians, as monotheists, could not accept the normal ancient assumption that some extra gods could be added to the list without undue tensions arising. As a result, the Jews could only sacrifice *on behalf of* the Emperor not *to* him; and the Christians refused to participate in any sacrifice at all.[20] There is no reason to think that they would have found it any easier to sacrifice to the traditional gods than to the Emperor, but since altars to the Emperor featured close to the tribunal of the magistrate who heard their cases, it was a symbolic sacrifice to the Emperor that was usually asked of them to prove their renunciation of their Christian loyalty. Another area of tension seems to have been the attitude of some élite members, who found difficulty or at least irony in accepting the treatment of a man as a god. This means that we have some wry, bitter humour at the Emperor's expense, but even this is not as simple to interpret as it might seem to be. The most famous essay of this kind is a satire probably written early in the reign of Nero by Seneca, when he was a leading adviser to the young Emperor.[21] The satire is at the expense of Claudius, the new god and recently dead Emperor, and it can be read as a savage attack on the deification of rulers in general; but, in fact, the joke is more complicated than that. The satire features speeches by many of the gods assembled in their own senate; but the main attack on the proposed new god comes not from Jupiter or the other traditional gods of Rome, but from no less a god than *Divus* Augustus himself; he attacks the idea of deifying Claudius, not of course on the grounds that deifying human beings is in itself ridiculous, but that Claudius was too ridiculous a human being to be honoured by deification.[22]

[20] The Jews were only able to sacrifice at all until the destruction of the temple at Jerusalem after the revolt of AD 66–70: Philo, *Embassy to Gaius* 155–8 = *RoR* ii.**12.6c(ii)**; *RoR* i.341; Christians and sacrifice: Gordon (1990); Rives (1995); *RoR* i.225–6; ii.**6.8**.

[21] Seneca, *The Pumpkinification of Claudius* (*Apocolocyntosis*); cf. Griffin (1976), 129–33; commentary by Eden (1984).

[22] The point of the satire rests on layers of irony, so that it is risky to make any inferences as to the author's attitude to the worship of Emperors as such; perhaps *Divus* Augustus too is being made fun of.

For the most part, there seems to have been little inhibition through-out the Empire on accepting that the living Emperor should be treated as a god, and only very spasmodic efforts were made by the Emperor himself to reject such offers of worship. It seems only to have been in Rome itself that this was not acceptable. There alone, a great ceremony grew up which took place after the Emperor's death and which turned on the idea that the apotheosis took place after death and only to some Emperors, not to all. There is even talk of a witness who appeared in the senate, where approval of the ritual always took place, and testified that the Emperor's soul had ascended in the form of an eagle. In other cases, the dead Emperor was never deified and consequently received no posthumous cult at all.[23] The distinction between the gods, the *Divi* (the dead deified), and the living Emperor and his wife (the not-yet-deified) is carefully marked in the sacrificial records of the Arval Brethren:

. . .an ox to Jupiter, a cow to Juno, a cow to Minerva, an ox to *Divus* Augustus, a cow to the *Diva* Augusta ⟨i.e. Livia⟩, an ox to *Divus* Claudius, a cow to the *Diva* Poppaea Augusta, a bull to the *Genius* of the Imperator Nero Claudius Caesar Augustus Germanicus ⟨i.e. Nero⟩, a cow to the Juno of Messalina ⟨i.e.Nero's wife⟩. [24]

So the list follows a consistent order: first, the old gods; secondly, the *Divi*; thirdly, the *Genius* and Juno of the living ruler and his wife. There is careful respect for the rule that living rulers do not receive sacrifice directly as gods; and that the sacrifices to their divine essences take the lowest place in the ritual order. But we have no reason to think that this precision had to be respected outside the Roman context. However, the same distinction of victims for the *Divi* and the *Genius* of the ruler was still being respected almost two centuries later in a military calendar preserved at the remotest edge of the Empire on its Eastern frontier, where the *Divi* still receive their oxen, the *Divae* their cows, and the living Emperor of the day (Severus Alexander, AD 222–235) has a bull sacrificed to his *Genius*, exactly like Nero.[25] Clearly for the specialists in the cultic niceties of Roman practice, about which great care was taken, these distinctions were of the greatest importance; but equally clearly, they belonged to Rome and official Roman institutions such as the army,

---

[23] For the ceremonies, Price (1987); *RoR* ii.**9.3b**; after Caesar and Augustus, Claudius was the next to be deified, so that Tiberius and Gaius were omitted, as later Nero and Domitian. Fourteen Emperors were deified in all between Augustus and Caracalla. For a table, based on the Arval records, Scheid (1998a), 133.

[24] Scheid (1998a).

[25] Fink (1971) = *RoR* ii.**3.5**, under June 26.

and there was no attempt to impose them in the provinces. So far as Roman religion itself is concerned, therefore, we have consistent evidence over the whole period of the Republic and into the Imperial period that a great deal of fluidity and creativity was acceptable about the gods, goddesses, and rituals of Rome.[26]

[26] On which see Beard (1985).

VII. NEW FORMS

It is easy to think that pagan religion was essentially tolerant of other forms of religious activity. The evidence we have just considered seems at first sight to support just such an interpretation. If the Romans could accept a steady flow of new cults into their city over such a long period of time, that must surely imply that their attitudes were basically tolerant. There are, however, qualifications to be made before reaching such a conclusion. It is clear that, if there was tolerance, it was not tolerance born of principle. So far as we know, there was no fixed belief that a state or an individual ought to tolerate different forms of religion; that is the idea of far later periods of history.[1] The truth seems to be that the Romans tolerated what seemed to them harmless and drew the line whenever there seemed to be a threat of possible harm; only, they saw no great harm in many cults of their contemporary world, where many individuals and cities worshipped gods and goddesses much like their own.

This becomes very clear in the 180s BC when they do meet a cult, that of Bacchus, which for some reason they decide to treat as a threat to their own order. Our knowledge of these events is based on slender evidence, in the form of a text of the senate's decree regulating the cult and a long account by Livy, rich in many ways but far from straightforward or reliable.[2] However, a picture of what happened does emerge from these rather unpromising sources. The cult was evidently not a new one; it had deep roots in Italy and was closely related to a traditional local cult, that of Liber Pater.[3] Even the particular form of Bacchus cult found in the 180s was quite obviously well established already. We hear of it as a familiar cult in the plays of Plautus performed in Rome many years before the 180s;[4] and archaeological evidence has made it even more certain that the Roman authorities must have had a clear knowledge of the cult long before they launched their persecution of it.[5] Even the decree controlling the cult contains a clause to regulate what should

---

[1] North (1979).
[2] The decree is *ILS* 18 = *ILLRP* 511 = *RoR* ii.**12.1b**. Livy's text is 39.8–19 (partly translated at *RoR* ii.**12.1a**). Massive discussion and full bibliography to 1988, Pailler (1988); North (1979); Gruen (1990), 34–78; Walsh (1996).
[3] Bruhl (1953).
[4] North (1979), 88; Gruen (1990), 50–51.
[5] *RoR* i.93.

happen if a particular Bacchic group possessed a shrine with sacred objects in it. For Livy, however, there is no question of any such advance knowledge. His whole narrative is a tale (presumably a fiction) of how the consul of the year 186, by his ingenuity and persistence, discovered this plot, broke the news of it to a senate aghast at the discovery and duly took dramatic action to suppress it, not just in the Roman area but throughout Italy.[6] Such a persecution is, so far as we know, quite unprecedented for Rome and must imply that the authorities perceived a major threat in the character of the cult. But what was the threat?

There are various theories. One is that this was not a religious crisis at all, but simply a case of police action against a conspiracy to commit ordinary crimes. Another is that the cult was seen as a foreign influence at a period when the Romans were highly suspicious of Greek influence on their culture. These ideas are not necessarily wrong, but they seem inadequate to explain either the scale of the witch-hunt throughout Italy or the sudden assault on a cult previously accepted; and they can all too easily be explained away as part of the propaganda against the cult rather than the senate's real objection to it.

The crucial clues come in the senate's decree passed at the time, which we possess on a bronze tablet, which was found in S. Italy in a form addressed, not to Roman communities themselves, but to one of the allies, quoting the decree as drafted for the allied communities as a whole. The regulations are entirely concerned with the structure of the groups on which the cult organization was evidently based. It forbids the groups to have leaders, or male priests, or a group fund, or oaths of allegiance; it also restricts the size of groups and the structure of their membership.[7] This only makes sense on two assumptions: first, that the senate was banning the group organization that they knew existed throughout Italy; secondly, that they were dealing, not with a wild and sudden irruption of uncontrolled fanaticism, but with a well-established highly structured form of cult. If this is true, then there is no need to invoke either foreign influence (the cult may well have had deep local roots) or fear of criminal activity, though both were of course useful tools in the propaganda war that must have taken place against a dangerous religious enemy.

The existence of groups such as these implies a major change in the religious culture of Italy at this period. The accounts we have make it

---

[6] Livy, above n. 2, esp. 14–15.

[7] The details of the decree's contents are well analysed by Tierney (1947); see North (1979); a different view in Gruen (1990), 34–78.

clear that the cult was very widespread, in Rome itself, in the Rome area, in Etruria, and in central and southern Italy. At this date Italy was far from being a single people or culture and the implication is that its appeal cut across the lines of political and social control.[8] The authorities of Rome would have been familiar with a situation in which religion followed and expressed the main lines of the city's social structure. State cults were organized by the state; family cults by the (always male) head of the family; the cults of particular sections of the city or country by the local authorities in the regions; and clubs based on work or neighbourhood by their own chosen leaders. But what is to us the most familiar form of religious organization, that is through religions or sects, consisting of members joined by shared religious beliefs, is virtually unknown in the cities of the Graeco-Roman world. So there was no alternative power system consisting of churches and priests to stand against political assemblies and councils. The organization of the Bacchic groups must therefore have struck the Romans as both new and dangerous to established modes of power.

The analogy with the far later persecution of the Christians should not be pressed too far. There is no reason to think that the worshippers of Bacchus were in any way hostile to the gods and modes of worship of the societies in which they lived. They did not, as did the later Christians, reject sacrifice or regard the pagan gods as demons. They presumably would have had no problem in attending pagan rituals or respecting gods other than their own. But the threat was all the same seen as real: Livy, even though he was writing long after the events, gives us some idea of what was at stake, in a speech (composed by himself) that he gives to the consul of the time, Postumius Albinus, speaking at a popular assembly (*contio*) and warning them of the threat of a rival power:

Unless you take precautions, men of Rome, this day-time assembly of yours, properly summoned by the consul, could come to be rivalled by their night-time assembly. At the moment they, separately, fear you, all together in an assembly; it is when you have all scattered back to your homes and farms, that they will assemble to take counsel about their own salvation and your destruction. It is then that you, separately, will need to fear them, all together.   (Livy 39.16.4)

In some ways, in fact, the action against the adherents of Bacchus was far more determined and consistent than was that against the Christians centuries later. There is simply no question here of waiting for individuals to be denounced to the authorities; the state's officials and

---

[8] *RoR* i.92–6.

soldiers went out to seek the cult-members and put large numbers of
them to death.

It is difficult to exaggerate the importance of the religious revolution
of which this development was the first sign in Italy. Once a society has
within it groups of people who have joined together because of their
shared religious beliefs, a whole new set of religious possibilities arises.
The leadership of the group acquires a degree of control that priests had
previously lacked; the organized group becomes a potentially threaten-
ing force in politics; beliefs, which had been scarcely considered important in the traditional context, become the focus of great interest and
attention, because the individual's beliefs have become for the first time
the critical determinant of his or her religious location; conversion from
one religion to another becomes a possibility for the first time; and as a
consequence the individual begins to be identified as a member of a
particular group. The most conclusive development of all is when the
members of a group start to share a common name and to be universally
known by that name. In the case of the Bacchus-worshippers of the 180s
BC there are traces of this development: at least the women members of
the cult are known as Bacchae and men of respectable status, whatever
their origins (Roman citizen, Latin or allied), are forbidden to consort
with them, unless given specific permission from Rome. Whether the
implication of the name is that the adherents of the cult saw themselves
as exclusively 'Bacchists', and therefore cut off from the normal belief in
the pagan gods, our sources do not tell us and we should not assume that
they do.

In the longer run, the consequence of this new kind of religious life
must have been very radical. A series of new elements follow on: for the
first time, the individual is asked to take decisions in the course of his or
her life that deeply affect their experience and their religious commit-
ments. These decisions need not have been dramatic; there is no need to
evoke the model of a sudden conversion like those of the great saints of
the Christian tradition, though those do supply us with the most extreme
cases we know of.[9] Again, not all the decisions will have been genuinely
individual, because often a family, even including the family's slaves, will
have had little choice but to follow the decision of the head of the family,
and perhaps some of those who might have changed their allegiance
were not brave enough to defy the family's authority. But there is no
doubt that in the period of the Roman Empire there must have been

---

[9] On these, see the classic work of Nock (1933).

many cases of individuals who changed their religious allegiance because they had changed their beliefs. These events, as they became familiar, must have changed the social significance and meaning of 'beliefs', which had previously hardly mattered or been challenged. It must have been as a result of all this that individuals start to take their own experience far more seriously as a trigger to religious action.[10]

The revolution in religious behaviour that follows in the course of subsequent centuries consists of two related processes that are effectively the two sides of a single transformation. Their effects are felt throughout ancient society, both by those who are the actors in the changes and by those who are not. The short-term effects could sometimes be violent, though very seldom as violent as the suppression of the Bacchic cult in the 180s BC, which is why that period remains so significant and its interpretation so tantalizing; more often we see a pattern of slow change, gradual accommodation, some intellectual confrontation, and very little open conflict. The fate of the Bacchus cult itself is not known after the disastrous events of the 180s BC: it is clear that the idea and imagery of the cult remained and that Bacchic groups did continue to exist or were later revived in some forms, but we hear of no more trouble with them in the late Republic.[11] An echo of the cult's mysteries exists still in the decorated room of the Villa of Mysteries at Pompeii; but it is not agreed at all whether this should be seen as a decorative scheme or as a reference to the cult's practice in the house.[12]

We can identify other groups of religious activists in the following period, who are the objects of limited, but hostile action by the Roman authorities. Chaldaeans (i.e. presumably astrologers) were expelled from Rome in 139 BC, supporters of Isis on various occasions in the late Republic in the early principate; Jews, possibly in 139 BC, together with the Chaldaeans, and certainly later.[13] In all these cases, we can assume that at least part of the problem would have been that the practitioners of these cults or arts were seen as foreigners involved in un-Roman actions. The actions against them seem to have been far less violent and sustained than that against the Bacchus worshippers had been, more by way of being temporary police action than serious

---

[10] North (1992a).
[11] For an Imperial Bacchic group of some kind, Scheid (1986).
[12] Seaford (1981); Henderson (1996); *RoR* i.161–4.
[13] Incident of 139 BC: Valerius Maximus 1.3.2. Isis cult: *RoR* i.161; 230–1; Jews: Josephus, *Jewish Antiquities* 18.65–84; Tacitus, *Annals* 2.85.

persecution. But that may be precisely because they were seen as foreign groups, not as a mixture of socially varied origin brought together by their beliefs. Foreigners with odd habits might have seemed dangerous but could be far more easily dealt with than deviant groups of locals.

In the centuries that followed, a number of cults, generally and evocatively, though inaccurately, known as Oriental Mystery Cults, attracted supporters in Italy and the Western Empire. The name is misleading because the cults in question did not share their Eastern elements in common; they did have (or at least claim to have) elements from various parts of the East – Isis from Egypt, Cybele and Attis from Asia Minor, Atargatis from Syria, Mithras from Persia, and so on.[14] The problem is not just that some of these claims seem to be flimsy, but that at least some of the cults in fact have a similar structure involving an initiation ritual, the revelation of secret knowledge to the initiates, and continuing membership of a group. This common structure can be shown clearly to derive from early Greece, not from the East at all.[15] So, it seems very likely that these cults evolved in Greek cultural contexts in different parts of the Hellenistic World, using the indigenous deities of the different areas and the idea of the wisdom of the East to construct new religious forms, which evidently had their greatest appeal to Westerners not Easterners. The Roman Empire will have provided the possibilities of travel and trade, which enabled both people and religions to travel widely.

The problem that has long provoked the most theorizing and specu-lation is the relationship between the existence of these pagan cults and the emergence in much the same period of even more radically new religious forms, such as Judaism, Christianity, and Manichaeism. The simplest theory was that as traditional pagan worship declined and was increasingly abandoned by the Romans themselves, the mystery cults provided a step in the 'right' direction; they catered for spiritual needs that the traditional cults had failed to meet, but did not go far enough. We saw earlier that the basis of such theories lay in a deep misconcep-tion about the character of traditional civic pagan worship.[16] The underlying idea goes back to a nineteenth-century developmental theory, which regarded Christian monotheism as a higher evolutionary stage, inevitably destined to replace inferior forms of worship.[17] On this

[14] General accounts: Burkert (1987); Smith (1990); Turcan (1996); *RoR* i.263–312.
[15] So, Burkert (1987).
[16] Above, pp. 29–32.
[17] See Scheid (1987), 311–12; North (1997).

view (which still has its defenders) it was just a question of time before pagans saw the inadequacy of their own outlook.

There are, however, some respects in which it is possible to argue that the pagan mystery cults did share some common ground with Christianity. They must have offered their initiates a more personal experience than the sharing in community cult, which was characteristic of older rituals. They also gave admission to a group of members, linked by some permanent organization, with its own priests and leadership. In some versions, we can also find what seem to be highly significant convergences between Christian and pagan experience. So, for instance, in his famous attack on the behaviour of women, Juvenal, the second-century AD Roman satirist, describes with the greatest contempt the commitment of a female devotee of the goddess Isis to her worship: she is willing to undergo the most terrible suffering for the sake of the goddess and even to accept the intervention of the priests of the cult in her married sexual life.[18] What is important here is not Juvenal's predictable hostility, but the religious activities that he despises and can hardly have invented and which are not at all what we would have expected to find in a pagan context. Again in the context of the Isis cult, but this time from Apuleius' novel *The Golden Ass*, we have another account of religious experience going outside the limits usually supposed to apply to pagan life; the source is problematic, if only because it is a novel, and an elusive, playful novel at that; but whatever the author's attitude (arguably quite derisive) towards the cult, it is not believable that the experiences of his hero are totally divorced from the possibilities of real life. If so, they offer a glimpse of the experience of an initiate into the mysteries of the goddess.The hero, Lucius, in gratitude for the goddess' help seems to devote himself to her service; he receives spiritual advice and guidance from the priest; he is visited by the goddess in a dream; he receives three initiations under her inspiration and has his whole life transformed by the experiences he undergoes. It would be risky to classify this as a 'conversion' in the full sense, because we have no way of knowing whether Lucius rejects his 'pagan' past, but we leave him utterly devoted to the goddess' service, though also as a successful lawyer in Rome.[19]

In the earlier part of the twentieth century, it was fashionable to make

---

[18] Juvenal, *Satire* 6.522–41 = *RoR* ii.**12.4d**.
[19] On the interpretation of Apuleius: Nock (1933), 138–55; Griffiths (1975); Winkler (1985); *RoR* ii.**12.4b**; on the Isis cult: Burkert (1987); Versnel (1990); Turcan (1996); on the role of women in the cult Heyob (1975), but with some caution.

a further suggestion, viz. that the mystery cults offered their initiates a secure place in the afterlife and that this transcendence of death was in all cases foreshadowed by the death and re-birth of the deity of the cult.[20] It was argued further that this pattern of religious expression was originally a pagan pattern long antedating the emergence of the Christian version. It started from the worship of vegetation gods, dying in the winter and reborn each spring. Christianity was then created by the mixing up of the Jewish idea of the Messiah and the pagan idea of the god that dies to create immortality for his followers. This idea has been criticized from many points of view and would be difficult to defend in this form today.[21] For one thing, the different mystery cults do not all seem to offer the prospect of a life after death and even if they do it is far from clear whether they were already doing so before the development of Christianity. Each of them seems rather to have had its own pattern of revealing a mystery and rewarding its initiates. So for instance the myth of Attis seems to end not in the re-birth of the god, but only in a partial and inadequate recovery, which must support a quite different eschatology.[22] Meanwhile, Mithraism has another quite different pattern of experience, in which the progress of the initiate through different phases of revelation seems to be mirrored by the progress of the soul through stages in the celestial sphere.[23]

There are also important limits to the degree of convergence. The pagan cults never, so far as we know, separated from the mainstream of pagan life. Adherents had no need to reject the other gods or to avoid the festivals and rituals of the city cults or the practice of emperor worship. So there was nothing that necessarily brought them into conflict with the authorities, and mystery cults even occasionally received support from members of the élites.[24] The most one can say is that some of their proceedings were supposed to be secret and that the meeting-places of the worshippers of Mithras were not in public spaces but in private rooms. It is also possible that we should look below the surface of the Mithraic cult and ask how far it might have been in conflict with normal pagan beliefs, at least in some of its manifestations. This might seem astonishing in a cult that was so prominent in the context of the army in frontier areas, where it seems likely to have been a semi-official cult, with

---

[20] For discussion, Sfameni Gasparro (1985).
[21] For critical studies, Brandon (1963).
[22] Sfameni Gasparro (1985).
[23] Beck (1988), 73–85; Turcan (1996), 224–43: *RoR* ii.12.5.
[24] *RoR* i.291–3.

its grades of initiation reflecting the ranks of the army.[25] But a cult that was not only all-male, but classified women as outside humanity,[26] and whose central emblem of the bull-sacrifice by the god seems to have been designed to break all the normal conventions of animal sacrifice,[27] can hardly have co-existed too comfortably with normal city life. But there is no evidence of any conflict, beyond the fact that leading Romans who played a part in the cult in the army seem not to have advertised any commitment back in Rome.

One of the major limitations on the writing of the religious history of the Roman Empire is that the histories of pagan religion, of Judaism, especially that of the Diaspora Jewish communities, and of Christianity have often been written by specialists in these different disciplines without attempting to look for the interactions between them. If we could be sure that they both originated and operated in isolation from one another there would be no great harm done by this; but in fact it is clear that by the second to third centuries AD communities of all three and of other groups as well co-existed in mutual awareness in Rome and in many other cities of the Empire. What is more, Christianity at least started as a tiny group, essentially a variant form of dissident Judaism; as it grew, it did so in each generation by persuading pagans or Jews to join Christian groups.[28]

From the point of view of this book, the most important religious phenomenon to be noted is the emergence of various ideas and institutions which arise from the contact of different religious groups – conversion, persecution and martyrdom, heresy, and the credal statements which become necessary to define and repress them.[29] If these conceptions had existed at all before, they would have had very limited application in relation to the pagan religion of the city, when the citizen was not presented with alternative religious possibilities. The nearest approach we know of is the situation discussed at the beginning of this chapter, when a form of religion is certainly persecuted; as we have seen there is no evidence that the Bacchus-worshippers were intentionally cutting themselves off from pagan religion, but at least potentially they could have moved in that direction and perhaps the Roman authorities feared that they were doing so.

---

[25] Gordon (1972); *RoR* i.294–5.
[26] Gordon (1980).
[27] For an example: *RoR* ii.**12.5b**. Vermaseren (1963), 67–106.
[28] Relation with Judaism: Lieu, North, Rajak (1992); Christian development: Hopkins (1998).
[29] Conversion: Nock (1933); martyrdom: Frend (1965); Bowersock (1995); creeds: Kelly (1972).

At much the same period, Jewish groups in the cities of both the Greek and Roman worlds were, we know, maintaining their own religious traditions while living in cities that were operating as pagan communities.[30] That implied keeping a different calendar and a different diet from the other members of the community and, at least in principle, avoiding the rituals and festivals of the pagan city. This would not necessarily lead to conflict or persecution, though it always might do so.[31] But it does imply that all the inhabitants must have become aware of the existence of groups who lived inside, but refused the religious traditions of, the city where they lived. Such Jewish Diaspora communities were, however, not offering a potential threat to city life, because their religion was inherited from their ancestors, and they did not seek vigorously to convert their neighbours to their practices.[32] They would not therefore have seemed radically different from the other ethnic groups, who also lived in pagan cities and maintained their own religious lives. The pagans might think them odd or funny, but hardly menacing.

In some respects, this was perhaps an error. Just like the later communities of Christians, the Jews did in fact reject the gods and goddesses of the gentiles. Moreover, Jewish communities do seem to have attracted followers who attached themselves to the synagogues in the cities where they lived and gave support to the Jewish religious life.[33] It is also true that Jewish religious identity was in the end incompatible with the practice of another religion, though that is not to say that individuals did not try to maintain their Judaism as well as attending pagan rituals. The truth is that we do not know the life of Jews in pagan cities well enough to judge how this was done. However that may be, in other respects Christian groups as they developed proved to be far more objectionable to Roman authorities than did Jewish ones.

The persecution of the Christians by the Roman authorities is both like and unlike the Bacchanalia persecution from which this chapter started: like, because both occasions seem to cause radical action, in defiance of the normal patterns of pagan life; unlike, because the persecution of the Christians seems to have been so erratic and uncertain by comparison with that of the Bacchus-worshippers. The context is not just a few years in Italy, but two centuries over the whole Roman Empire; the practice of Christianity does seem to be held to

[30] *RoR* ii.12.6.
[31] Rajak (1992); Goodman (1992).
[32] For conversion to Judaism, or the lack of it, see Goodman (1992); (1994).
[33] For 'godfearers': Rajak (1992), 20–21; Reynolds and Tannenbaum (1987).

imply culpability throughout this period and the authorities certainly had the power to take violent action whenever they wanted to do so. We know that the Roman governors, at least when dealing with ordinary provincials who did not possess Roman rights, could put them to death if they refused to renounce their Christianity, and there certainly were occasions when this happened.[34]

The Emperor Trajan gave a famous ruling that the Christians were not to be sought out, but only punished if they were denounced by an accuser who gave his name and could therefore be punished if the accusation turned out to be unfounded.[35] This was a relatively liberal position and, although we cannot be sure whether it was always applied consistently, it does seem certain that there was no methodical attempt to stamp out the new cult. However, it does need to be recalled that Trajan's ruling only implied toleration if the Christians remained discreet and self-contained, not if they made any attempt to convert pagans, which would inevitably lead to conflict and to denunciations. The actual evidence we do have consists for the most part, though not entirely, of accounts in the so-called martyr-acts:[36] these are accounts by Christians of the heroism of the early martyrs, often told in the form of an account of the trial and of the punishment of the martyrs, with a great deal of emphasis on the torture to which they were subjected. It is of the greatest interest and importance that this new genre is invented at this point and the type of the martyr (originally one who bears witness) is an important new element in religious vocabulary, apparently produced simultaneously in Jewish as well as in Christian writings.[37] It is, however, very difficult to be sure of the date and historical reality of the acts, even though some of them seem factual and may be quite reliable.

If it is a problem to establish the frequency of persecutions, it might seem that the same could be said also of conversions.[38] We know in any detail about only a small number of conversions and although these too imply the invention of a new category of religious experience, direct evidence of frequency simply does not exist. However, we need to remember that the sudden dramatic conversion of a Saul/Paul or an Augustine is only one possible form of the movement of individuals from one group to another. Allowance has to be made for far less

---

[34] Sherwin White (1963), esp. 1–23.
[35] Pliny, *Letters* 10.96–7 = *RoR* ii.**11.11b**.
[36] Musurillo (1972); Bowersock (1995), 23–39.
[37] For the dating of the Jewish martyrdom accounts in Maccabees, Bowersock (1995).
[38] Nock (1933); *RoR* i.275–6.

dramatic changes of view, either by individuals on the basis of their own decisions or by whole families on the authority of the head, the *paterfamilias*. Such conversions from pagan to Christian (or perhaps back) would not have attracted attention, unless they became the focus of a denunciation. That such events took place, even though we lack individual cases, cannot be doubted. The Christians started as a tiny group of loyal members, many of them staying within the community of Jews and retaining their commitment to the temple cult and respecting the Law. The expansion of this tiny nucleus took many decades and implies a progressive annual expansion of their numbers. Most of that expansion must have been the result of many decisions by unknown individuals, who had previously been pagans. It follows that a high percentage of the Christians at any date between AD 70 and AD 250 must have been converted rather than born into the new faith. They were pagans by origin, learning the new way of living.[39]

It is by no means necessary for us to think that this slow process was invariably accompanied by protests and conflict.[40] There must have been long periods in which pagans, Jews, and Christians lived together in the same cities without any conflict. On the other hand, the combination of the high authority of the pagan *paterfamilias* with the Christians' desire for converts must always have implied some threat of denunciations. The apparent rarity of serious conflicts suggest very strongly that many pagans took Pliny's view[41] that the Christians were harmless if over-superstitious and were therefore slow to provoke any serious action against them. The pattern only changes in the third century AD, when action at last becomes more centralized and more determined..

Even taking this cautious view of persecution, there are still questions to be asked about what did happen and why it happened: we should not forget that in the period covered by this book the Christians did not secure spectacular success; it is not yet appropriate to speak of the triumph of Christianity, when their progress was still so slow and so uncertain. Why then did they arouse such hostility? There is no shortage of possible answers: the Christians are sharply distanced from their contemporaries in various ways and it is always possible that these differences were enough in themselves to explain the occasional out-break of conflict, even if there was no real threat to pagan life. The

---

[39] Hopkins (1998).

[40] Drake (1996) paints a plausible picture, though mostly dealing with later periods.

[41] Above, n. 35: 'I discovered nothing worse than a depraved and excessive superstition'.

Christians believed in one god and, more significantly, denied the gods and goddesses of the rest of mankind; they resisted pressure to perform the simplest act of worship; they met in groups and maintained group organization. Any of these characteristics might have given rise to suspicion; but it is still hard to believe that they would have been enough had the Christians been a clearly foreign group like the Egyptians or the Syrians. The search for a serious cause for fear must surely take us back to the issue of conversion.

The real conflict must have happened within families, not just in the public arena. Amongst the rather thin sources we have for this early period is a tale of conflict preserved in the writings of the Christian apologist Justin.[42] A wife was converted to Christianity against her husband's will and as a result started to refuse to sleep with him. He took his revenge by denouncing to the authorities the man who converted her. Granted that at any date in our period, the Christians would have been largely quite recent converts, their fellow-citizens would have known them as the children or grandchildren of pagans. The conclusion that we have to come to is that at the heart of the confrontation between pagans and Christians must have lain tensions within family groups of pagans and ex-pagans. This is a phenomenon that did not exist at all in the earlier years of the Empire.

[42] Justin, *Second Apology* 2 = *RoR* ii.12.7f(I).

VIII. READING PAGAN TEXTS

As the argument of the last chapter suggested, one level at which religious change had its most profound and lasting effects was in the character of the language used in religious discourse. This has a double impact on our understanding: first, it is one of the key areas in which we can see religious change taking place; but, secondly, understanding the different uses of language is a precondition of interpreting the different religions themselves. The Christians spoke a far more direct language about the character of the deity, the character of priesthood, about the beliefs that an individual ought to hold or not hold and about the character of the interaction between divine and earthly beings. To some extent, the pagans were forced into making explicit statements by way of competition; but, far more clearly, we should regard them as disadvantaged in the competition with Christianity by the nature of their own traditions of religious discourse. It is easy but dangerous to jump from this observation about pagan habits of speech to making simplifying assumptions about their religious experience. Just because they are inexplicit and guarded in what they say, we have no right to assume that they were either hypocritical or uninterested in regard to the gods and goddesses they worshipped or that the rituals they carefully maintained and practised carried no meanings for them.

It is important to remember that both the Romans themselves and the Greeks who came to observe them in the later Republican period regarded the Romans as the most religious of peoples. The Romans themselves announced this to the Greek world: already in the 190s BC, when receiving a mission from the men of Teos, they reply:

We <Romans> have totally and consistently held reverence towards the gods as of the highest importance and the truth of this is proved by the favour we have received from them in return. We are also quite sure that our great respect for the divine has been evident to everybody. As a result of these factors, and because of our goodwill towards you and towards the envoy who presented your request, we declare your city and its territory holy (as it is already), inviolable, and free from Roman taxation.

$(SIG^3 \ 601, 12–20)$

The Teans were not at this date under Roman authority, so the document is an extraordinary mixture of religious modesty, ascribing all their achievements to the gods, and human arrogance, in assuming the right to confer benefits and freedom from interference.[1] The same theme of Roman religious supremacy is emphasized half a century later in a very different context by the Greek historian Polybius,[2] when set to explain the superiority of the Romans over the peoples (including his own) that they had defeated in war. The crucial difference between the Romans and their rivals for imperial success was, he argues, the respect the Romans show for matters of ritual and religious practice. For Polybius, admittedly, this is a matter not so much of praise for the piety of the Romans, as of criticism for the failure of the Greeks; and he regards it as a failure not because he is himself a religious man (far from it), but because he thinks of religion as a tool of social control to be used by the ruling élite, and one that the Greeks have forgotten how to use. We can, however, accept his evidence about the religious reputation of the Romans without accepting his biased interpretation of it. In fact, he contradicts himself by his own examples, which suggest that Roman leaders were themselves pious rather than cynical manipulators of their own religion.[3]

It is in reading texts such as Livy's version of Roman history that we can look most hopefully for more sense of what the Romans understood by their own religiousness. Very rarely, if ever, does Livy abandon the position of attributing proper religious behaviour to the old Romans and allowing criticism to arise only when he reports bad behaviour on the part of individuals, especially of those who came to a bad end or lost major battles.[4] There is a strong tradition in modern writing that nevertheless sees Livy as sceptical in religious matters, so that normally he states the official position on any point, but just occasionally drops his guard and allows his real disbelief to slip through. This view of Livy is, however, far from secure and rests on the interpretation of a few controversial remarks, all on the assumption that the untypical case is the give-away. This issue is still in need of clarification, but what is clear is that the practice of Livy and later historians is to conceal their own thoughts for the most part; to report the activities of men and treat a historical narrative as a man-made construction; but also to give space and credence to the role of the gods, while seldom, if ever, stating a direct intervention.

In saying this, however, we have to remember that Livy was writing

---

[1] North (1993).
[2] Polybius 6.56.6–14. = *RoR* ii.13.1.
[3] He implies that the Roman leaders were trusted because they respected their own oaths.
[4] Rosenstein (1990), 54–91.

his Roman history after the fall of the Republican system, with a consciousness that the great achievements of the Romans of the past belonged to a lost system and a lost moral order. He could never forget, of course, that Augustus claimed to be restoring these lost traditions and, not least, the lost religious traditions, but that does not make him blind to the fact of change. In one passage he seems to refer explicitly to the new practices as opposed to the old, when he apologizes – or pretends to apologize – for including in his history the annual prodigy lists:

I am well aware that, through negligence that arises from the popular belief that the gods do not give portents of the future, prodigies are no longer either publicly announced or included in the annals. All the same, for me when I am writing about old-time matters the mind becomes in some way ancient itself, and also a certain religious inhibition (*religio*) prevents me from treating as unfit for inclusion in my annals events that the wisest of the men of that age thought should be publicly dealt with.

(Livy 43.13.1—2)

Where does this leave him? He implicitly criticizes the 'modern' negligence that derives from popular scepticism; and yet he implies that he would be willing to follow the fashion of other recent historians, except that some kind of religious reticence holds him fast to the traditional way. Critics have interpreted this all too often as if it were a statement of simple scepticism; simple it certainly is not. It might almost be safer to take the meaning as the opposite: Livy *would* come into line with his fashionable contemporaries, he says with false modesty, except that they are being so careless, so ignorant and so unimaginative in their interpretations that he could not conceivably do so. But it is also important to remember that he is speaking not about his private beliefs, but about the proper style for a Roman historian dealing with the practices of the past.

This observation of Livy's is instructive not least because it reminds us how hard it is for us today to understand the thoughts of pagans about their religion. It is at this point that modernizing assumptions are at their most seductive, tempting us into seeing total scepticism or a modern 'scientific' outlook on the basis of a criticism aimed at some particular event or idea. As a matter of methodology, the safest starting point for such an interpretation is to regard belief in the gods as virtually universal among the Romans, even though they may have differed as to how and when the gods did or did not influence human activities. Like any other, this assumption will sometimes mislead us, but it will do so far less frequently than does the obsessive search for modern sceptical attitudes in ancient men and women.

One type of text may seem to challenge this argument straight away: that is, philosophical writings and, above all, those of Cicero in the last years of his life. In his *On Divination (de divinatione)* and *On the Nature of the Gods (de natura deorum)* he has left us two discussions of issues concerning the gods, both of which contemplate philosophical positions radically inconsistent with the practices of the Roman cult, including those for which Cicero, as an augur and a proud one, was himself responsible. In the first, one of two speakers defends divination as a reality and the other attacks it as an illusion. In the second, a range of philosophical views is discussed as to whether the gods exist and whether they influence human life. In neither of the two does Cicero in his own person reject the negative view or express adherence to the positive one. We can then be certain that these were matters of debate among the reading élite of Rome in Cicero's day. As a matter of fact, the views must have been current far earlier, since they are those of the Greek schools, Epicureans and Stoics, which would have been familiar much earlier than Cicero, even though he was famously the first to write philosophy in Latin.[5] It is also highly relevant that he was himself at this point writing as a member of the Academy, which involved him, as understood at this period, in refusing to decide the issue for his readers, but leaving the decision to them after hearing a balanced argument.[6]

The problem here is not to work out Cicero's views, though that is difficult in itself, but to know what inferences we can make about the religious life of the Romans, or perhaps of the Roman élite, from the existence of these debates. It is certain (a) that intellectuals often tend to exaggerate the impact of their kind in past periods; and (b) that reading the views of, say, Bertrand Russell on Christianity would not by itself allow us to recontruct the religious history of twentieth-century Britain. It would, in my view, be a crude oversimplification to argue that philosophical debate must have undermined belief in the gods even for Cicero himself, let alone for those of his contemporaries who read his work or the great majority that did and could not.

If then these philosophical tracts should be left on one side as evidence of religious activities and views, the key evidence comes from a wealth of literary evidence of other kinds: the historians, as we have already seen, but also poets, novel-writers, essayists, satirists, and not least the *Natural*

---

[5] The Romans chose to make a public rejection of philosophy at intervals in the second century BC: for discussion, Gruen (1990), 170–92.

[6] For the significance of this see discussions on the interpretation of Cicero's *On Divination*: Linderski (1982); Momigliano (1984a); Beard (1986); Schofield (1986); *RoR* ii.**13.2**.

History of the elder Pliny. For most of these, religion is not in itself a theme of debate, but a natural and inevitable part of all themes of debate. The most directed work we have, on which a good deal of attention has been focused recently, is the *Fasti* of the Augustan poet Ovid, which is an extended discussion of the religious calendar, written in the last years of Augustus' long reign and the beginning of that of Tiberius, when Ovid was still hoping to be recalled from his exile.[7]

At first sight, the poem seems to be an assembly of miscellaneous information, some of it the same as is conveyed by the inscribed calendars of the Augustan period, but also calendrical and astronomical information added by Ovid himself.[8] But the central material consists of explanations of the festivals and rituals of the year, some, but not all, tied to particular dates. Much of the explanation takes the form of myths and stories. To take a typical example, when Ovid is discussing the Lupercalia:

You ask why do the Luperci run? and why (for this is the custom) do they strip themelves and run with their bodies naked?
The god <Pan> himself takes pleasure in running swiftly in the high mountains and it is he who inspires sudden flights.
The god himself is naked and orders his followers to go naked too. For running, clothing is unsuitable.
The Arcadians are said to have occupied their lands before Jupiter was born and their race to be older than the moon.

(Ovid, *Fasti* 2.283–90)

He goes on to say that the Luperci preserved a memory of these primitive Greek customs, from a time before clothes were invented. But this explanation turns out to be only one of a series. There follows a distinctly crude little story, still set in Greek mythology, to account for the god's dislike of clothes, which had once deceived him into making a public laughing stock of himself by mistaking Hercules for a woman, and then without apology:

My Muse, add Latin reasons to these foreign ones; and let my horse run in its native course.

He then goes on to a story of Romulus and Remus, who happened to be practising athletics naked, when they were called on to rescue their flocks. The naked runners preserve the memory of this exploit.[9]

[7] On the *Fasti*: Newlands (1995); Feeney (1998), 123–33.
[8] The point is made by Feeney (1998),126–7.
[9] See above, p. 47.

At one level, this should all be seen as a display of knowledge that provides its own justification. To be learned on the religious antiquities of Rome means to know the traditions and stories and know them as well as anyone else, or better. It evidently is not a matter of establishing a single truth, because there could be endless versions of the truth. Nor is it important to produce a native Roman explanation, but rather to distinguish the Greek from the Roman while re-telling both. The Greek stories and elements seem to be fully accepted as part of the Roman reality; sometimes, but not always, the Greek stories are racier than the Roman ones, but that is not a consistent principle.[10] One familiar device is for the narrator of the *Fasti* to use a god or goddess as his interlocutor, and even these informants also sometimes offer (tongue in cheek, of course) different theories about their own rituals. It should not be missed that much of this display of learning is light-hearted and witty and we should never for a moment be lured into thinking that the first-person claims of the narrator ('I too have jumped through the fires set three in a row . . .') should be taken seriously as autobiographical for him, let alone for Ovid himself. The humour of the *Fasti* ranges from great crudeness to the most delicate play, and this too is a problem for modern readers who tend to regard religion as by definition un-funny. If it is a witty, learned poem, then it cannot also (they think) be a commentary of any significance on the rituals of the calendar.[11] This is exactly the assumption that we should most mistrust and challenge; but once again it is the lack of the straightforward religious language that is puzzling to the modern reader.

If there are serious problems in reading Roman pagan writings on religion and recognizing how they are expressing their attitudes towards the gods and towards human communications with the gods, the problems become worse still when the writings of pagans come to us, as is often the case, through the medium of Christian polemic against the pagans.[12] Such polemic often takes the form of long quotations from pagan authors, in particular from the antiquarians of the late Republic and early Empire who were a mine of detailed information about cults and their practices, and whose writings were still available to Christians such as Arnobius of Sicca, Lactantius, and Augustine. Their contribution of these quotations to our knowledge is important, sometimes

---

[10] On this issue, Phillips (1992); Parker (1993); Newlands (1995).
[11] For the relationship of religion and humour see Berger (1997).
[12] Liebeschuetz (1979), 252–77; Markus (1970), 45–71.

crucial, but it sets real problems of assessing and allowing for their biased attitudes.

For example, Augustine (*City of God* 6.10) quotes a passage from an essay on superstition by the early imperial writer Seneca. In part he summarizes him, in part seems to quote word for word (but is he being careful?). The impression conveyed is that Seneca is attacking pagans in general; and the passage is important for us because it gives us a picture of ritual activity normally not mentioned in pagan sources:

> Jupiter has one special attendant to announce visitors and one to tell him the time; one to wash and another to oil him, who as a matter of fact is only miming the hand movements. Juno and Minerva each have a special female hairdresser, who works at some distance not just from the statue but from the temple; these mimic the finger-movements of hairdressers, while others again hold up mirrors. You find people praying to the gods to put up bail for them; and still others handing over writs and expounding the lawsuits they are engaged in.
>
> (Seneca, On Superstition, fr. 35–7 [Haase])

There is no doubt of the dramatic location of all this – the Capitoline Hill in front of the triple temple of Jupiter, Juno, and Minerva, the site of the most prestigious of all Roman religious actions. Augustine's use of Seneca's text is intended to give the impression that this was an attack on pagan religion as such by a leading pagan authority, describing what went on in the very heart of imperial pagan Rome. In fact, it seems clear that this is a distortion by Augustine; the passage starts (before the part cited above) by attacking a foreign ritual (the cult of Osiris) and moves on to more common superstitions. So Seneca is making the quite common distinction between proper religion (*religio* – a virtue) and excess of piety *(superstitio* – which becomes a vice).[13] He is attacking popular expressions of piety from a Stoic viewpoint and characterizing them as superstitious. The point is quite important because the text gives us a most unusual glimpse of a level of pious belief in the old gods and goddesses, and ritual practices not known from elsewhere. It also leaves us with an open question as to whether this is simply traditional but otherwise unattested ritual behaviour, or whether it is new development in Seneca's own day, responding to a changing aspect of the pagan gods in the course of the first century AD. For the gods and goddesses here seem to be taking a personal role in the lives of their devotees – and this is years before we can imagine Christianity having any influence on pagan religious behaviour.

---

[13] For *religio* and *superstitio*, see *RoR* i.ch 5.

The best way of illustrating the difference is to compare pagan with Christian modes of speech. Consider, for instance, the confidence of Augustine (*City of God*, 15.25) discussing the actions of God at the time of the flood – had God really changed his mind about the human race?

The anger of God is not a mental disturbance; it is a judgement to impose punishment on sin. For him, consideration and re-consideration are the application to issues that are subject to change of a plan that is itself unchanging. God never repents of any action, as do men, and his resolution is absolute about any matter whatsoever, because he has certain foreknowledge.

For Roman pagans, the motivations and activities of the gods and goddesses were not to be summarized and asserted in this direct way, but at most implied or referred to in veiled language. But the lack of directness should not be mistaken for doubt about their existence; only about our capacity to read their thoughts correctly, or perhaps about the possible dangers of being too confident in speech.

Recent discussion has emphasized one particular means of expressing the difference between pagan Roman religious experience and the later forms with which we are familiar today and which have their roots, at least, in the life of the Roman Empire. The particular means is to say that religion was then a matter of ritual, not of belief. At one level, this theory provides us with an explanation of the differences discussed in this chapter. Rituals can be said to convey meanings and to do so very powerfully, but they do not translate into agreed verbal forms; different participants at different times may have quite different experiences of the same ritual, both being equally valid.[14] It is not therefore surprising – on this theory – if ancient religious language is discreet, coded and, to our way of thinking, even evasive. To put your fears and hopes based on the gods into the language of causation and action was to make it too explicit, even dangerously explicit.

Modern interpretations of the role and nature of rituals broadly support the idea that it can occupy a central role in the culture and functioning of a wide range of human societies.[15] Once it can be shown that the Romans were seriously engaged with it and had a tradition of reflection and discussion about it, it becomes realistic to think of making progress in using the evidence we have to improve our grasp of the value and meaning of the religion. However, the danger of this theory is also quite clear and turns on yet another confusion between pagan and later

---

[14] So Feeney (1998), 117–21.
[15] For a recent theory, Rappoport (1999).

ways of thinking about religion. For us of the twenty-first century, to perform rituals but not to hold and express the beliefs that correspond to the rituals is to be a hypocrite, seeking the social benefits of conformity, while concealing any inconvenient scepticism. Nineteenth- and twentieth-century discussions are full of this assumption, applied confidently to the Romans, as if it were a universal truth. Cicero, for example, is said to continue to behave in public as if he were a 'believer', when his philosophical writings give the game away; or still worse, it is argued that philosophical writngs show that he had had a conversion experience and lost his beliefs.[16] All this seems to rest on confusions about the terminology used.

It is easier to define what we should not do in seeking to understand Roman rituals than to discover how to establish any framework of interpretation for them. So, for instance, it seems clear that we should not try to decode rituals in any straightforward way; that we must not assume that rituals had a single main interpretation that could be discovered even in principle; least of all, that to establish the origins of the ritual will reveal an unchanging inner meaning which will illuminate its significance at any particular date. Similarly, it is a mistake to overemphasize any question of the participants' belief or disbelief in the efficacy of ritual actions, when we have no access to their private thoughts and good reason to suspect that the whole problem derives from later not pagan preoccupations. Another reason why it must be a mistake to think that rituals can be translated into language is because they are often not statements about the world, but actions that in themselves change the state of the world (by constituting changes of status, or appeasing the gods, or starting or ending states of war etc.). These rituals are not saying things, but doing things.

On the other hand rituals, at least of the Roman type, are by their very nature not the inventions of any known person, but conceived as endlessly repeated with the cycle of time or of repeated events; that is why, when they do change, the change has to be veiled. Consquently, we can say that rituals should always be seen in relation to shared ideas about the past of the city; the fact that they have always happened and are always to be repeated evokes the past and forms a link between the past and the present, so that the performing of the rituals not only calls up and defines the identity of the Romans, but even in some senses constitutes it.

---

[16] Momigliano (1984a).

These are all controversial issues and there will certainly continue to be arguments about the interpretation of difficult texts and the right approach to them. This is however an area in which progress has been most marked in the recent past and to which a good deal of attention should be paid in future. There are three approaches to be noted: the first is the application to Roman religion of modern theories about ritual and the relation of rituals to religious life;[17] the second is the sensitive analysis of such ritual texts as we have, especially those of the Arval Brethren, which are potentially very rich direct sources;[18] thirdly, the analysis of Roman poetry, which has many reflections of ritual life, not often taken seriously enough.[19]

This book has aimed to summarize and report on some fundamental changes in our way of looking at the religious life of Roman pagans. It is not claiming to provide a complete new vision of their experience, but rather to open up new approaches to texts, to the interpretation of rituals, to ancient art and archaeology, the understanding of which has been blocked in the past by expectations inappropriate to the Romans' time and place. The claim will only be tested by the progress that may be made, or not made, in the future.

[17] See (e.g.) Phillips (1986); Versnel (1990, 1993).
[18] Scheid's edition (1998a) of the texts should renew debate on the significance of the best material we have for analysing continuity and change in Roman practice.
[19] Feeney (1998).

BIBLIOGRAPHY

1. Abbreviations

ANRW = *Aufstieg und Niedergang der römischen Welt,* edd. H. Temporini and
W. Haase (Berlin, 1972–).
BEFAR = Bibliothèque des Ecoles françaises d'Athènes et de Rome.
BICS = *Bulletin of the Institute of Classical Studies.*
CP = *Classical Philology.*
EPRO = Etudes préliminaires sur les religions orientales dans l'Empire romain.
(Leiden, 1961–).
HTR = *Harvard Theological Review.*
JRH = *Journal of Religious History.*
JRS = *Journal of Roman Studies.*
MAMA = *Memoirs of the American Academy at Rome.*
MRR = Broughton (1951–2).
PBSR = *Papers of the British School in Rome.*
PCPS = *Proceedings of the Cambridge Philological Society.*
PdP = *Parola del Passato.*
P & P = *Past and Present.*
RoR = Beard, North, Price (1998).

2. List of Works Cited, and Further Reading

Altheim, F. (1938): *A History of Roman Religion* (London).
Ampolo, C. (1988): 'Rome archaique: une société pastorale', in C.R. Whit-
taker, ed., *Pastoral economies in classical antiquity* (Cambridge).
Beard, M. (1980): 'The sexual status of Vestal Virgins', *JRS* 70, 12–27.
—— (1985): 'Writing and ritual: a study of diversity and expansion in the Arval
Acta', *PBSR* 53, 114–62.
—— (1986): 'Cicero and divination: the formation of a Latin discourse', *JRS*
76, 33–46.
—— (1987): 'A complex of times: no more sheep on Romulus' birthday',
PCPS 213, n.s. 33, 1–15.
—— (1989): 'Acca Larentia gains a son: myths and priesthood at Rome', in
Images of Authority (Camb.Phil.Soc., Supp. 16), eds. M.M. Mackenzie and
C. Roueché, 41–61 (Cambridge).

—— (1990): 'Priesthood in the Roman Republic', in Beard and North (1990), 17–48.

—— (1994): 'The Roman and the foreign: the cult of the "Great Mother" in imperial Rome', in *Shamanism, History and the State*, eds. N. Thomas and C. Humphrey, 164–9 (Ann Arbor).

—— (1995): 'Re-reading (Vestal) virginity', in *Women in Antiquity*, eds. R. Hawley and B. Levick, 166–77 (London and New York).

Beard, M. and Crawford, M.H. (1985): *Rome in the Late Republic* (London).

Beard, M. and North, J.A. eds. (1990): *Pagan Priests* (London).

Beard, M., North, J.A., and Price, S.R.F. (1998): *Religions of Rome*. 2 vols. (Cambridge) (= *RoR* i and ii).

Beck, R. (1988): *Planetary Gods and Planetary Orders in the Mysteries of Mithras* (EPRO 109) (Leiden).

Belier, W.W. (1991): *Decayed Gods: Origin and Development of Georges Dumézil's idéologie tripartite'* (Leiden).

Benko, S. (1984): *Pagan Rome and the Early Christians* (Bloomington).

Berger, P. (1997): *Redeeming Laughter* (Berlin and New York).

Bernstein, F. (1998): *Ludi publici: Untersuchungen zur Entstehung und Entwicklung der öffentlichen Spiele im republikanischen Rom* (*Historia* Einzelschriften 119) (Stuttgart).

Bickerman, E.J. (1973): '*Consecratio*' in *Le culte des souverains dans l'Empire romain* (Fondation Hardt, Entretiens 19), 3–25 (Vandoeuvres-Geneva).

Bowersock, G.W. (1990): 'The pontificate of Augustus', in K. Raaflaub and M. Toher, eds., *Between Republic and Empire: interpretations of Augustus and his Principate* (Berkeley).

—— (1995): *Martyrdom and Rome* (Cambridge).

Brandon, S.G.F. (1963): *The Saviour God: Comparative Studies in the Concept of Salvation* (Studies presented to E.O. James) (Manchester).

Bremmer, J. and Horsfall, N. (1987): *Roman Myth and Mythography* (BICS Supp. 52) (London).

Broughton, T.R.S. (1951–2): *The Magistrates of the Roman Republic* (New York) (*MRR*).

Brown, P. (1988): *The Body and Society. Men, Women and Sexual Renunciation in Early Christianity* (New York).

Bruhl, A. (1953): *Liber Pater, origine et expansion du culte dionysiaque à Rome et dans le monde romain* (BEFAR 175) (Paris).

Burkert, W. (1987): *Ancient Mystery Cults* (Cambridge MA and London).

Cannadine, D. and Price, S. eds (1987): *Rituals of Royalty: Power and Ceremonial in Traditional Societies* (Cambridge).

Capdeville, G. (1995): *Volcanus: recherches comparatistes sur les origines du culte de Vulcain* (Rome).

Claridge, A. (1998): *Rome* (Oxford Archaeological Guides) (Oxford).

Coarelli, F. (1983–5): *Il Foro Romano* (2 vols.) (Rome).

Cornell, T.J. (1995): *The Beginnings of Rome: Italy and Rome from the Bronze Age to the Punic Wars (c.1000–264 BC)* (London).

Crawford, M.H. (1974): *Roman Republican Coinage*. 2 vols. (Cambridge).

—— (1996): *Roman Statutes*. 2 vols. (BICS Supp. 64) (London).

de Ste. Croix, G.E.M. (1963): 'Why were the early Christians persecuted?', *P & P* 26, 6–38 = *Aspects of Ancient Society*, ed. M.I. Finley, 210–49 (London and Boston MA).

Diels, H. (1890): *Sibyllinische Blätter* (Berlin).

Dorcey, P.F. (1992): *The Cult of Silvanus: a Study in Roman Folk Religion* (New York).

Drake, H.A. (1996): 'Lambs into Lions: exploring Early Christian intolerance', *P & P* 153, 3–36.

Dumézil, G. (1941–5): *Jupiter Mars Quirinus*. 3 vols. (Paris).

—— (1968–73): *Mythe et épopée*. 3 vols. (Paris).

—— (1970): *Archaic Roman Religion* (Chicago).

Eden, P.T., ed. (1984): *Seneca, Apocolocyntosis* (Cambridge).

Elsner, J. (1991): 'Cult and sacrifice: sacrifice in the Ara Pacis Augustae', *JRS* 81, 50–61.

—— (1995): *Art and the Roman Viewer: the Transformation of Art from the Pagan World to Christianity* (Cambridge).

Feeney, D.C. (1992): '*Si licet et fas est*: Ovid's *Fasti* and the problem of free speech under the principate', in *Roman Poetry and Propaganda in the Age of Augustus*, ed. A. Powell, 1–25 (London).

—— (1998): *Literature and Religion at Rome: Cultures, Contexts and Beliefs* (Cambridge).

Fink, R.O. (1971): *Roman Military Records on Papyrus* (American Philological Association), no. 117.

Fishwick, D. (1987–): *The Imperial Cult in the Latin West* (EPRO 108) (Leiden).

Fox, M. (1996): *Roman Historical Myths: the Regal Period in Augustan Literature* (Oxford).

Frend, W.H.C. (1965): *Martyrdom and Persecution in the Early Church: a Study of Conflict from Maccabees to Donatus* (Oxford).

Gabba, E. (1991): *Dionysius and 'The History of Archaic Rome'* (Berkeley).

Gagé, J. (1955): *Apollon romain. Essai sur le culte d'Apollon et le développement du 'ritus Graecus' à Rome des origines à Auguste* (BEFAR 182) (Paris).

Gager, J.G., ed. (1992): *Curse Tablets and Binding Spells from the Ancient World* (New York and Oxford).

Gallini, C. (1970): *Protesta e integrazione nella Roma antica* (Bari).

Gardner, J.F. (1998): *Family and Familia in Roman Law and Life* (Oxford).

Goodman, M. (1992): 'Jewish proselytizing in the first century', in Lieu, North, Rajak (1992), 53–78.

—— (1994): *Mission and Conversion* (Oxford).

Gordon, R. (1972): 'Mithraism and Roman society', *Religion* 2, pt. 2, 92–121 (repr. in Gordon (1996)).

—— (1980): 'Reality, evocation and boundary in the mysteries of Mithras', *Journal of Mithraic Studies* 3, 19–99 (repr. in Gordon (1996)).

—— (1987): 'Aelian's Peony: the location of magic in the Graeco-Roman tradition', in *Comparative Criticism*, ed. E.S. Shaffer, 9, 59–95 (Cambridge).

—— (1990): 'The Roman Empire' (chs. 7, 8, and 9) in Beard and North (1990), 177–255.

—— (1996): *Image and Value in the Graeco-Roman World* (Aldershot and Brookfield VT).

Graf, F. (1997): *Magic in the Ancient World* (Cambridge MA and London).

Grant, M. (1973): *Roman Myths* (Harmondsworth).

Griffin, M.T. (1976): *Seneca: a Philosopher in Politics* (Oxford).

Griffiths, J.G. (1975): *Apuleius of Madauros. The Isis-Book (Metamorphoses Book XI)* (EPRO 39) (Leiden).

Gros, P. (1976): *Aurea Templa. Recherches sur l'architecture religieuse de Rome à l'époque d'Auguste* (Rome).

Gruen, E.S. (1990): *Studies in Greek Culture and Roman Policy* (Cincinnati Classical Studies 7) (Leiden).

Hanson, J.A. (1959): *Roman Theater-Temples* (Princeton).

Harmon, D.P. (1978): 'The public festivals of Rome', *ANRW* II.16.2, 1440–68.

Henderson, J. (1996): 'Footnote: representation in the Villa of the Mysteries', in *Art and Text in Roman Culture*, ed. J. Elsner (Cambridge).

Heurgon, J. (1957): *Trois études sur le 'ver sacrum'* (Coll. Latomus 26) (Brussels).

Heyob, S.K. (1975): *The cult of Isis among Women in the Graeco-Roman World* (EPRO 51) (Leiden).

Holleman, A.W.J. (1974): *Pope Gelasius I and the Lupercalia* (Amsterdam).

Holloway, R.R. (1994): *The Archaeology of Early Rome and Latium* (London).

Hopkins, K. (1983): *Death and Renewal* (Cambridge).

—— (1991): 'From blessing to violence', in *City States in Classical Antiquity and Medieval Italy*, ed. A. Molho, 479–98 (Stuttgart).

—— (1998): 'Christian number and its implications', *Journal of Early Christian Studies* 6.2, 185–226.

—— (1999): *A World Full of Gods: Pagans, Jews and Christians in the Roman Empire* (London).

Judge, E.A. (1980–1): 'The social identity of the first Christians: a question of method in religious history', *JRH* 11, 201–17.

Kelly, J.N.D. (1972): *Early Christian Creeds* (3rd edn.) (London).

Koch, C. (1937): *Der römische Juppiter* (Frankfurt).

—— (1960): *Religio: Studien zur Kult und Glaube der Römer* (Nurenberg).

Kraemer, R.S. (1992): *Her Share of the Blessings: Womens' Religions among*

Pagans, Jews and Christians in the Greco-Roman World (New York and Oxford).

Kyrtatas, D.J. (1987): *The Social Structure of the Early Christian Communities* (London and New York).

Lane Fox, R. (1986): *Pagans and Christians* (Harmondsworth and New York).

Latte, K. (1960): *Römische Religionsgeschichte* (Handbuch der Altertumswissenschaft, V.4) (Munich).

Le Bonniec, H. (1958): *Le culte de Cérès à Rome de l'origine à la fin de la république* (Etudes et commentaires 27) (Paris).

Levene, D.S. (1993): *Religion in Livy* (Mnemosyne Supp. 127) (Leiden).

Liebeschuetz, J.H.W.G. (1979) *Continuity and Change in Roman Religion* (Oxford).

Lieu, J., North. J., and Rajak T., eds. (1992): *The Jews among Pagans and Christians in the Roman Empire* (London and New York).

Linderski, J. (1982): 'Cicero and Roman divination', *PdP* 37, 12–38 (= Linderski (1995), 458–84).

—— (1986): 'The augural law', *ANRW* II.16.3, 2146–312.

—— (1995): *Roman Questions* (Stuttgart).

Liou-Gille, B. (1980): *Cultes "heroiques" romains; les fondateurs* (Paris).

MacBain B. (1982): *Prodigy and Expiation: a Study in Religion and Politics in Republican Rome* (Collection Latomus 177) (Brussels).

Markus, R.A. (1970): *Saeculum: History and Society in the Theology of St Augustine* (Cambridge).

Meeks, W.A. (1983): *The First Urban Christians: the Social World of the Apostle Paul* (New Haven and London).

Mellor, R. (1975): Thea Rome: *the Worship of the Goddess Roma in the Greek World.* (Hypomnemata 42) (Göttingen).

Michels, A.K. (1967): *The Calendar of the Roman Republic* (Princeton).

Miles, G.B. (1995): *Livy: Reconstructing Early Rome* (Ithaca and London).

Millar, F.G.B. (1984): 'The political character of the Classical Roman Republic, 200–151 BC', *JRS* 74, 1–19.

Moatti, C. ed. (1998): *La mémoire perdue* (CEFR 243) (Rome).

Momigliano, A.D. (1984a): 'The theological efforts of the Roman upper classes in the first century BC', *CP* 79, 199–211 = *Ottavo contributo* 261–77 = Momigliano (1987), 58–73.

—— (1984b): 'Georges Dumézil and the trifunctional approach to Roman civilisation', *History and Theory* 23, 312–30 = Momigliano (1987), 289–314.

—— (1987): *On Pagans, Jews and Christians* (Middletown).

Musurillo, H. (1972): *The Acts of the Christian Martyrs* (Oxford).

Nash, E. (1976) *Pictorial Dictionary of Ancient Rome* (2nd ed.) (London).

Newlands, C.E. (1995): *Playing with Time: Ovid and the Fasti* (Ithaca and London).

Nock, A.D. (1933): *Conversion* (Oxford).

—— (1952): 'The Roman army and the Roman religious year', *HTR* 45, 186–252 = Nock (1972), ii.736–90.

—— (1972): *Essays on Religion and the Ancient World* 2 vols. (Oxford).

North, J.A. (1975): 'Praesens Divus' [Review of Weinstock (1971)], *JRS* 65, 171–7.

—— (1976): 'Conservatism and Change in Roman Religion', *PBSR* 44, 1–12.

—— (1979): 'Religious Toleration in Republican Rome', *PCPS* 25, 85–103.

—— (1986): 'Religion and politics, from Republic to Empire', *JRS* 76, 251–8.

—— (1990a): 'Family strategy and priesthood in the late Republic', in *Parenté et stratégies familiales dans l'antiquité romaine*, eds. J. Andreau and H. Bruhns, 527–43 (Rome).

—— (1990b): 'Diviners and divination at Rome', in Beard and North (1990), 51–71.

—— (1992a): The development of religious pluralism', in Lieu, North, Rajak (1992), 174–93.

—— (1992b): 'Deconstructing stone theatres', in *Apodosis. Studies presented to Dr W.W. Cruickshank*, 75–83 (London).

—— (1993): 'Roman reactions to Empire', *Scripta Classica Israelica*, 12, 127–38.

—— (1995): 'Religion and rusticity', in *Urban Society in Roman Italy*, eds. T.J. Cornell and K. Lomas, 135–50 (London).

—— (1997): 'The religion of Rome from Monarchy to Principate', in *Companion to Historiography*, ed. M. Bentley, 57–68 (London and New York).

Orlin, E. (1997): *Temples, Religion and Politics in the Roman Republic* (Leiden and New York).

Pailler, J.-M. (1988): *Bacchanalia: la répression de 186 av. J.-C. à Rome et en Italie* (BEFAR 270) (Rome).

Palmer, R.E.A. (1974): *Roman Religion and the Roman Empire: Five Studies* (Philadelphia).

Parke, H.W. (1988): *Sibyls and Sibylline Prophecy in Classical Antiquity* (London).

Parker, H.C. (1993): '*Romani numen soli*: Faunus in Ovid's *Fasti*', *TAPA* 123, 199–217.

Phillips, C.R. (1986): 'The sociology of religious knowledge in the Roman Empire to A.D. 284', *ANRW* II.16.3, 2677–773.

—— (1992): 'Roman religion and literary studies of Ovid's *Fasti*', *Arethusa* 25, 55–80.

Potter, D.S. (1994): *Prophets and Emperors: Human and Divine Authority from Augustus to Theodosius* (Cambridge MA and London).

Price, S.R.F. (1984): *Rituals and Power: the Roman Imperial Cult in Asia Minor* (Cambridge).

—— (1987): 'From noble funerals to divine cult: the consecration of Roman Emperors', in Cannadine and Price (1987), 56–105.

Rajak, T. (1992): 'The Jewish community and its boundaries', in Lieu, North, Rajak (1992), 9–28.

Rappoport, R. (1999): *Ritual and Religion in the Making of Humanity* (Cambridge).

Rawson E. (1971): 'Prodigy lists and the use of the Annales Maximi', *CQ* 21, 158–69 = Rawson (1991), 1–15.

—— (1973a): 'Scipio, Laelius, Furius and the ancestral religion', *JRS* 63, 161–74 = Rawson (1991), 80–101.

—— (1973b): 'The interpretation of Cicero's *de legibus*', *ANRW* I (1973),334–56 = Rawson (1991), 125–48.

—— (1974): 'Religion and politics in the late second century BC', *Phoenix* 28, 193–212 = Rawson (1991), 149–68.

—— (1976): 'The first Latin annalists', *Latomus* 34/5, 689–717 = Rawson (1991), 245–71.

—— (1985): *Intellectual Life in the Late Roman Republic* (London).

—— (1991): *Roman Culture and Society. Collected Papers* (Oxford).

Reynolds, J.M. and Tannenbaum, R. (1987): *Jews and Godfearers at Aphrodisias* (Cambridge, Philological Society, Supp. 12) (Cambridge).

Richardson, L. jnr. (1987): *A New Topographical Dictionary of Ancient Rome* (Baltimore and London).

Rives, J.B. (1995): *Religion and Authority in Roman Carthage from Augustus to Constantine* (Oxford).

Rose, H.J. (1948): *Ancient Roman Religion* (London).

Rosenberger, V. (1998): *Gezähmte Götter: das Prodigienwesen der römischen Republik* (Stuttgart).

Rosenstein, N.S. (1990): *Imperatores Victi: Military Defeat and Aristocratic Competition in the Middle and Late Republic* (Berkeley).

Rüpke, J. (1990): *Domi militiaeque: Die religiöse Konstruktion des Krieges in Rom* (Stuttgart).

—— (1995): *Kalender und öffentlichkeit: Die Geschichte der Repräsentation und religiösen Qualifikation von Zeit in Rom* (Berlin and New York).

Ryberg, I.S. (1955): *Rites of the State Religion in Roman Art* (MAMA 23) (New Haven).

Seaford, R.A.S. (1981): 'The mysteries of Dionysus at Pompeii', in *Pegasus: Classical Essays from the University of Exeter*, ed. H.W. Stubbs (Exeter).

Scheid, J. (1983): 'G. Dumézil et la méthode experimentale', *Opus* 2, 343–54.

—— (1985): *Religion et piété à Rome* (Paris).

—— (1986): 'La thiase du Metropolitan Museum', in *L'association dionysiaque dans les sociétés anciennes* (CEEFRA 89), 275–90.

—— (1987): 'Polytheism impossible; or, the empty gods: reasons behind a void in the history of Roman religion', in *The Inconceivable Polytheism* (History and Anthropology 3), ed. F. Schmidt, 303–25 (Paris).

—— (1990): *Romulus et ses frères. La collège des Frères Arvales, modèle du culte public romain dans la Rome des Empereurs* (BEFAR 275) (Rome).

—— (1992a): 'Myth, cult and reality in Ovid's *Fasti*', *PCPS* 38, 118–31.

—— (1992b): 'The religious roles of Roman women', in *A History of Women: from Ancient Goddesses to Christian Saints*, ed. P. Schmitt Pantel, 377–408 (Cambridge MA).

—— (1993): 'The priest', in *The Romans*, ed. A. Giardina, 55–84 (Chicago).

—— (1995): 'Graeco ritu. A typically Roman way of honouring the gods', *HSCP* 97, 15–34

—— (1998a): *Commentarii Fratrum Arvalium qui supersunt* (Roma Antica 4) (Rome).

—— (1998b): *La religion des romains* (Paris).

Schilling, R. (1954): *La religion romaine de Vénus* (BEFAR 178) (Paris).

Schofield, M. (1986): 'Cicero for and against divination', *JRS* 76, 46–65.

Schürer, E. (1973–87): *The History of the Jewish People in the Age of Jesus Christ*, rev. ed. G. Vermes, F. Millar, and M. Goodman. 3 vols. (Edinburgh).

Scullard, H.H. (1981): *Festivals and Ceremonies of the Roman Republic* (London).

Sedley, D.N. (1998): *Lucretius and the Transformation of Greek Wisdom* (Cambridge).

Sfameni Gasparro, G. (1985): *Soteriology and Mystic Aspects in the Cult of Cybele and Attis* (EPRO 91) (Leiden).

Sherwin White, A. N. (1963): *Roman Society and Roman Law in the New Testament* (Oxford).

Smith, J.Z. (1978): *Map is not territory. Studies in the History of Religion* (Leiden).

—— (1990): *Drudgery Divine. On the Comparison of Early Christianities and the Religions of Late Antiquity* (London and Chicago).

Stambaugh, J.E. (1978): 'The functions of Roman temples', *ANRW* II.16.1, 554–608.

Staples, A. (1998): *From Good Goddess to Vestal Virgins: Sex and Category in Roman Religion* (Leiden and New York).

Steinby, E.M. (1993–): *Lexicon Topographicum Urbis Romae* (Rome).

Szemler, G.J. (1972): *The Priests of the Roman Republic* (Collection Latomus 127) (Brussels).

Taylor, L.R. (1961): *Party Politics in the Age of Caesar* (Berkeley and Los Angeles).

Tierney, J.J. (1947): 'The senatus consultum de Bacchanalibus', *Proceedings of the Royal Irish Academy*, 57, 89–117.

Torelli, M. (1982): *Typology and Structure of Roman Historical Reliefs* (Ann Arbor).

Toynbee, J.M.C. (1971): *Death and Burial in the Roman World* (London).

Turcan, R. (1996): *The Cults of the Roman Empire* (Oxford).

Vermaseren, M.J. (1963): *Mithras, the Secret God* (London).

Versnel, H.S. (1970): *Triumphus* (Leiden).

Versnel, H.S. (1981): 'Self-sacrifice, compensation and the anonymous gods', in *Le sacrifice dans l'antiquité* (Fondation Hardt, *Entretiens* 27), 135–94 (Geneva).

—— (1990, 1993): *Inconsistencies in Greek and Roman Religion* (Studies in Greek and Roman Religion 6.1 and 6.2). 2 vols. (Leiden).

Wallace-Hadrill, A. (1987): 'Time for Augustus: Ovid, Augustus and the *Fasti*', in *Homo Viator: Classical Essays for John Bramble*, eds. M. Whitby et al., 221–30 (Bristol and Oak Park IL).

Walsh, P.G. (1996): 'Making a Drama out of a Crisis: Livy on the Bacchanalia', *G&R* 43, 188–203.

Warde Fowler, W. (1911): *The Religious Experience of the Roman People from the Earliest Times to the Age of Augustus* (London).

Wardman, A. (1982): *Religion and Statecraft among the Romans* (London).

Watson, A. (1993): *International Law in Archaic Rome: War and Religion* (Baltimore).

Weinstock, S. (1971): *Divus Julius* (Oxford).

Winkler, J.J. (1985): *Auctor & Actor. A Narratological Reading of Apuleius'* The Golden Ass (Berkeley).

Wiseman, T.P. (1974): *Cinna the Poet and Other Roman Essays* (Leicester and New York).

—— (1984): 'Cybele, Virgil and Augustus', in *Poetry and Politics in the Age of Augustus*, eds. T. Woodman and D. West, 117–28 (Cambridge).

—— (1995): *Remus. A Roman Myth* (Cambridge).

Wissowa G. (1912): *Religion und Kultus der Römer* (Handbuch der Altertumswissenschaft, V.4), 2nd ed. (Munich).

Zanker, P. (1988): *The Power of Images in the Age of Augustus* (Ann Arbor MI).

Ziolkowski, A. (1992): *The Temples of Mid-Republican Rome and their Historical and Topographical Context* (Rome).

ABOUT THE AUTHOR

John North studied at Oxford in the 1950s and wrote a thesis there under the supervision of Stefan Weinstock on the politics and religion of Rome in the middle Republican period. He came to University College London in 1963 as an assistant lecturer and has taught in the History Department there ever since, becoming a Professor of History in 1992. He has published articles and edited books on many aspects of the religious history of the Romans and is the author, together with Mary Beard and Simon Price, of *Religions of Rome* (Cambridge, 1998).

INDEX